SOCIETY AND THE HOMOSEXUAL

SOCIETY AND THE HOMOSEXUAL

by

GORDON WESTWOOD

with an Introduction by

DR. EDWARD GLOVER

GREENWOOD PRESS, PUBLISHERS
WESTPORT, CONNECTICUT

Library of Congress Cataloging in Publication Data

Westwood, Gordon.
  Society and the homosexual.

  Reprint. Originally published: New York :
Dutton, 1953.
  Bibliography: p.
  1. Homosexuality. I. Title.
HQ76.25.S46 1985   306.7'66   84-27933
ISBN 0-313-24840-0 (lib. bdg.)

*No part of this book may be reproduced
in any form without permission in writing
from the publisher, except by a reviewer
who wishes to quote brief passages in connection with a review written for inclusion in
magazine or newspaper or radio broadcast.*

Reprinted with the permission of Michael Schofield

Reprinted in 1985 by Greenwood Press
A division of Congressional Information Service, Inc.
88 Post Road West, Westport, Connecticut 06881

Printed in the United States of America

10 9 8 7 6 5 4 3 2 1

CONTENTS

Section I

THE EXTENT OF THE PROBLEM

Section II

THE CAUSES OF HOMOSEXUALITY

Section III

TREATMENTS AND CURES

Section IV

THE EFFECTIVENESS OF THE LAW

Section V

THE ATTITUDE OF SOCIETY

Section VI

LEVELS OF HOMOSEXUAL SOCIETY

7

Section VII

THE MIND OF THE HOMOSEXUAL

9

INTRODUCTION

Books purporting to inform the public on the psychology of sex fall naturally into two categories: those few which should find a conspicuous place on the family bookshelves, to be consulted when occasion demands by old and young alike, and that great majority which should be consigned forthwith to the waste-paper basket. This immediately raises the important question: how is the hapless reader, whose natural sexual curiosity is more often than not bedevilled by ignorance, uncertainty, anxiety, guilt and superstition, to determine into which category his latest purchase should fall? Hence the practice increasingly pursued by responsible publishers of securing a foreword to books on sexual subjects by someone who from the nature of his profession may be presumed to be sufficiently free from bias to go bail for the objectivity of the author.

Not that the possession of psychological, sociological or indeed medical qualifications is any guarantee that the writer of such forewords is himself free from moral prejudice or scientific bias. The history of the literature of sex is bestrewn with damaged reputations. Unchallenged authorities on physiology, psychology or for the matter of that on religion and moral philosophy have essayed the task of telling us what we ought to know about sex, only to produce in the great majority of instances textbooks which give evidence of less common sense than that presumably enjoyed by their most untutored readers. From the point of view of scientific prestige, the study of sexuality may well be scheduled as a dangerous trade.

Even when his scientific integrity and qualifications are beyond cavil, there is no reason to suppose that the most learned authority on some aspect or other of sexual activity is capable of writing a book suited to the needs of the general reader. The physiologist absorbed in the study of morphology and biochemistry may know little more of the psychology of sex than he has imbibed from the surreptitious reading of his nonage or from the exchange of arcana that goes on in the school dormitory or lavatory. The psychologist is not necessarily in much better case. If his concern is limited to the conscious aspects of sexual problems, he can do no more than draw tame and unilluminating conclusions: if on the other hand he is a clinical psychologist, familiar with the disorders that are due to unconscious sexual conflict, he is prone

11

to write a book that can be understood only by his more expert colleagues or at most by those sufferers from sexual maladjustment who are forced by bitter necessity to recognize the justness of his clinical findings. If he is a sociologist he can indeed supply us with interesting statistical data which shed much light on the sexual mores of the race, but little or none on the powerful forces that regulate unseen the sexual life of the individual. And if he be an exponent of religious morality, he starts his exposition of sex handicapped by supernatural preconceptions of human function that inevitably hamstring his scientific efforts. In short the common failing of the expert is that, setting out from his own particular nook, he proceeds to offer his readers *ex parte* instruction rather than to understand and meet halfway their most pressing needs.

In late Victorian and early Edwardian days the issue was simpler. Books on sex, including those by the great scientific pioneers, were frankly regarded as pornographic, saving always those publications, frequently written by retired clergymen, which sought to instruct different age-groups on what they ought to know, and ended either by causing alarm and despondency amongst their readers or providing the more enterprising of their youthful clientele with excitements that were none the less salacious because they were derived from admonitory sources. Now that the works of reputable sexologists are no longer confiscated as obscene literature, the position has changed, though not entirely for the better. A generation which has taken kindly to child guidance clinics and marriage guidance councils does not require much protection from pornography: but it does still require protection from bowdlerized information, confusion of counsel and crankiness masquerading as scientific teaching. The public has indeed a right to know that it is being given not only the facts, but a balanced assortment of facts such as will put sexual problems in a sane perspective.

The author of this book on homosexuality has clearly been guided throughout by these considerations. Mr. Westwood does not pretend to have written a clinical textbook of sexual disorder; nor, I think, would he venture to claim the status of a "psychologist of the unconscious." Still less does he ape the statistical preciosities of the sociologist. But, drawing on these and sundry other sources of information, he does attempt to give a balanced outline of the problem. And he does succeed more than most writers not only in setting homosexuality in proper perspective as a social as well as a sexual manifestation but also in conveying even to those whose knowledge of homosexuality is derived from music-hall jests, what manner of man the homosexual is,

12

his habits and social setting, his hopes and fears, his conflicts and aspirations. In this book the homosexual is not simply the *corpus vile* of the abnormal psychologist or the sexual offender beloved of the sociologist with a penchant for criminology; he is neither the moral reprobate committing mortal sin nor the pansy rousing the contempt, derision and often anger of the hearty but frequently inhibited heterosexual male. He emerges, unlikely as the conclusion may appear to some readers, as a man amongst men struggling in his own way, as they struggle in their own way, to deal with the problems and difficulties that arise from a combination of innate and developmental factors thrown into relief by the social milieu in which he must perforce exist. This is an achievement in presentation which deserves the attention of the thoughtful reader. Experts of various denominations may indeed find here and there views and opinions with which they may severally disagree, but they cannot gainsay the insight into the problem which the author displays or the skill with which he builds up his case.

For Mr. Westwood has a case. *It is in brief that homosexuality as commonly understood is not to be dismissed as the lecherous perversion of self-indulgent degenerates, but that it is one of the manifestations of a powerful unconscious force to which, in other forms, civilization owes much of its strength and some of the greatest of its achievements.*

Mr. Westwood does not rest this case solely on the facts that the cultural and æsthetic productivity of manifest homosexuals stands at a high level, that some of our finest intellects have been manifestly homosexual in tendency or that manifest homosexuals may exhibit an outstanding degree of ethical and moral responsibility. Borrowing from the discoveries of psycho-analysis he shews that unconscious bisexuality has the most fateful consequences both for good and for ill on man's behaviour. Under favourable circumstances, or, as the technical expression runs, when freely sublimated, unconscious homosexuality not only adds immeasurably to the cultural energies of mankind, but, in the modified and socially sanctioned form of friendship between persons of the same sex, is responsible for that cohesion and solidarity of social groups without which man would scarcely have risen above the level of the higher apes.

These are psycho-biological facts which the unoriented reader may find it difficult to credit. Accustomed to regard sexuality as a purely adult means of reproduction to which unique forms of physical and mental pleasure provide a compelling incentive, he cannot readily conceive that the sexual behaviour of the fully grown is but one functional outlet of forces which, from birth onwards, pervade every atom of his physical being and are active in every movement of his mind. Almost as difficult to believe is the plain fact that the mature forms of sexuality are a composite product, in which primitive infantile elements are merged and finally subjected to genital needs. Perhaps the dynamic situation created by these libidinal forces can more readily be grasped by imagining what would happen if the primitive and for the most part unconscious wells of sexual instinct were to dry up. The clamour of life would die away and the human race would fall gradually into a deep trance, disturbed by feeble and fitful efforts at food-getting. If, to follow a parallel train of thought, the homosexual components of man's instinctual inheritance could be singled out and de-sublimated, society as we now know it would gradually crumble to give place to a primitive organization in which jungle-law would once more prevail.

The validity of these broad assessments of homosexuality can be substantiated in the field of psychological medicine. Borrowing again largely from psycho-analytical sources, Mr. Westwood points out that mental disorders, ranging from slight characterological difficulties through the various neuroses to major mental disorders such as alcoholism and some of the insanities, can be traced in part at any rate to the conflicts arising from an (unconscious) state of imbalance of the homosexual instincts. These disorders, be it noted, occur most commonly, though not exclusively, in persons who are consciously free from any trace of manifest homosexual organization. Man has gained an uneasy ascendency over the more disruptive of his homosexual components, but it requires only a strong enough tip of the unconscious balance to throw him into states of mental illness or into manifest homosexuality.

Obviously then those who regard unconscious homosexuality as one of the great psycho-biological problems with which mankind is faced, are in a better position to view dispassionately, even sympathetically, the problem of handling manifest homosexuality. For if we are ready to regard at least some sexual deviations and perversions as "disorders" or "maladaptations", it would seem reasonable to enquire whether, like some other disorders of instinct, e.g., the common neuroses, they are amenable to modern methods of treatment. Unfortunately not all the factors in homosexual disorder are equally amenable to treatment; nor indeed should we insist on regarding all forms of manifest homosexuality as disordered states. Consequently we must be careful not to suggest either that treatment is an easy matter ending automatically in cure or that all forms of homosexuality are equally responsive to it. If we realize however that one of the most important factors leading to manifest homosexuality is that

14

of psychological upbringing, we are certainly in a better position to take important preventive measures.

Here again we must not jump to conclusions. It does not follow that manifest homosexuality is due solely to bad or misguided upbringing. In any case the tendency of children to identify with parents is a perfectly normal tendency on which normal development depends. We talk too readily nowadays of "mother-fixated boys." All boys are to some extent mother-fixated and so long as the fixation does not take on abnormal forms or exceed its optimum span of influence, there is no need for us to worry. But of course when the child is emotionally vulnerable or the parental policies misguided, the mother-fixated boy either may become manifestly homosexual or at any rate be left with an unresolved unconscious conflict over his homosexual leanings. It is at this point indeed that the most successful preventive measures can be applied.

But although the case for a sane and objective handling of the homosexual problem is already beyond question, we need be under no illusion as to the difficulties that must be overcome before the necessary organization is developed. For quite apart from popular opposition, we must expect a good deal of passive resistance from the Law, a faculty in which many of our most archaic moral prejudices are still enshrined. It is unquestionably the proper concern of the Law to preserve public decency, to protect both old and young from sexual seduction or assault either physical or mental; but it is no part of a sane Law either to confuse decency with prudery or to punish sick persons. It is equally certainly the duty of the State, through its services of child guidance and education and its organization of psychiatric facilities, to see that both preventive and curative measures are fully and freely available.

It is however not only the Law that obstructs progress in the handling of sexual problems. Even criminologists can be guilty at times of muddled thinking and, what is in the long run even more deplorable, of muddled investigations; for our researches on sexual problems are as yet only in their infancy. To many criminologists it seems quite natural that, since sexual offences bulk largely in criminal statistics, all sample investigations of crime should include their quota of sexual offenders. On the other hand it is the height of absurdity to draw conclusions about criminal types from statistics which include homosexuals of an ethical integrity often far above that of the average citizen. To be sure, the blind spots of the scientific investigator are among the more venial forms of prejudice, and, since for the time being the criminologist has little or no say in shaping the laws of the land, they are perhaps harmless enough. But the day is at hand when sexologists will exert an increasing advisory authority, and one cannot be too careful to scrutinize their commonsense as well as their credentials.

All of which brings us back to our starting point. The greatest obstacle to an objective understanding of sex problems lies in the moral prejudice, either conscious or unconscious, of the observer. Whether it manifests itself in the obtuseness of the scientist, in gales of music-hall laughter, in the harsh disapproval of the sexually inhibited "hearty," or the more pious reprobation of the moral philistine, the common prejudice regarding homosexuality can be traced to a common cause, namely, the tendency of the average man to castigate in others the impulses that lie hidden in his own unconscious mind.

EDWARD GLOVER.

Section I

THE EXTENT OF THE PROBLEM

CHAPTER I

IGNORANCE AND SECRECY

Some people would prefer to consider a problem to be solved by not recognizing it as a problem. This is especially true when the facts are unpalatable. Although we now live in a frank and realistic age, most people prefer to ignore the problem of homosexuality within our society. To many people it is no more than a subject for innuendoes and cheap sneers. If there is a more serious side to the problem, these people do not seem to be aware of it.

Yet in the larger towns it is difficult to understand how a man can avoid meeting the problem unless he is determined to turn a blind eye to it on every occasion. It is only necessary to visit any public lavatory in London to observe how numerous such practices must be. Nor is London unique in this matter. Every large town in Great Britain has its recognized street corners and public-houses where homosexuals can be sure they will meet others of their kind. One tavern in London is so well known that it has become almost a show place; celebrities who express a desire to see the night life of London are often taken to see this haunt of homosexuals.

When a visitor passes one of these street corners or enters one of these bars by mistake, he cannot fail to be aware of the fact that he is in a homosexual meeting place. Most people will leave as soon as possible. If they make any comment, it will be some harsh invective as if the mere sight has sullied them. Those visitors have stumbled upon the edge of a problem so large that no matter how much one may attempt to shroud it in secrecy, it must spill over into public life.

Occasionally when the homosexuals get too obvious or the place gets too infamous, the police will initiate a campaign to "clean up the town". But the police campaign is no more effective than beating a blanket to get rid of bed bugs. It is impossible to "clean up" these places because the problem is too large. All the police can do is to move them on, to spread the vice over a wider area.

Apart from these occasional police campaigns, the general

19

public go out of their way to avoid the whole subject. When it becomes impossible to avoid discussing the problem of homosexuality, the very word engenders any amount of blind prejudice and extreme emotional reaction. It is difficult to approach the problem with that complete detachment that is necessary to sort the facts from the superstitions.

The secrecy and moral indignation that surrounds this subject covers up the extent of the problem. The ordinary man thinks of a homosexual as an effeminate, over-dressed man with a high-pitched voice and a peculiar walk. But most homosexuals are not physically different from the normal man and are most careful to hide their abnormality from the rest of the world. For every recognizable homosexual that the public may see, there are many more hidden away from the unsympathetic eyes of the general public.

Even if the problem were limited to the street-corner loiterers and the underground homosexual societies of the big cities, they would still present a challenge to society to put its house in order. But they are only a small minority. Most of the homosexuals live and work among normal people and cannot be distinguished from normal people in any way. For the most part, they are decent, intelligent men as anxious to toe the social line as anyone. Physically they are exactly like their heterosexual fellows, but underneath there is the recognition that their tendencies are all against the law of the country and the moral code of our society. Inside there is a continuous emotional war, outside they guard the secret of their abnormality with a fearful tenacity.

Hundreds and hundreds of homosexuals never frequent the meeting places, do not know where they are, or would not wish to be seen near them. Some of them are married although they are true homosexuals in the sense that they are only sexually attracted to their own sex. It is often assumed that a man is complete heterosexual because he is married or is known to have had relations with the opposite sex. But homosexuality invokes such a strong social taboo that, even where there is no public knowledge of its existence, it cannot be assumed that these activities are not practiced.

Others find that marriage is impossible for them but they have had no overt homosexual experiences. Sir W. Norwood East[16] writes: "It is important to remember that perhaps the majority of homosexuals show little tendency to commit perverse acts on account of their high ethical standards. Homosexuality, as well as ordinary sexual behaviour, can develop on the highest plane."

But even those of the highest ethical standards do not escape the mental anguish or the feeling of guilt common to all homosexuals. During a correspondence in the *Spectator* on this subject, a clergyman pointed out that treatment is sometimes successful; he immediately received a flood of letters from all over Great Britain asking where such treatment could be obtained.[61] In fact those who repress their sexual needs for some ethical or moral reason are often found to be in a greater psychological tangle than the homosexual who has managed to adjust himself to his abnormality.

The results of homosexuality can lead to disgrace and ostracism, to pathological anti-social attitudes, or to severe neurotic conditions. These tragic results can occur when the homosexuality is overt or when it exists only in fantasy. So any study of the problem must include not only those who indulge in homosexual relations but also those who are attempting to divert or sublimate their homosexual impulses.

The dilemma is made much more difficult by the attitude of both homosexuals and heterosexuals. All but a few of the homosexuals are ashamed of their abnormality and are desperately anxious to hide away any manifestations of it from their fellow men. The rest of the community is either not prepared to discuss the subject at all, or views the whole business with a moral indignation which makes it impossible even to attempt a solution. As long as there is this conspiracy of silence on all sides, the true facts will never come to light and there can never be an understanding of the situation. And yet for hundreds of thousands of people in this country, and all over the world, it is an ever-pressing problem.

The only time that the problem comes out into the open is when a local or Sunday paper reports a recent court case in which the law has punished some individual for being a homosexual. If the man in the dock is a public figure who has made some notable contribution to the welfare of the community, the case may be reported with big headlines. The public always has enjoyed watching the fall of the mighty, but they never stop to enquire how an intelligent man could come to do such a meaningless thing.

Such a man may be immoral, he may be wicked, he may be diseased. Whatever he is, it is certain that he presents a problem that must be faced. In the last fifty years our civilization has made great progress in discussing sexual problems rationally and without emotion. We are now more enlightened about sex education, we are prepared to discuss the pros and cons of birth control, we recognize the importance of sexual compatability in marriage. None of these advances have been made without a long fight against the Victorian aftermath of timidity and evasiveness.

As recently as 1943 the powerful Newspaper Proprietors' Association bowdlerized the anti-V.D. campaign by the Ministry of Health, the Ministry of Information and the Central Council for Health Education. The original advertisement made three statements which were undoubtedly true, namely: "The first sign of syphilis is a small ulcer on or near the sex organs." "Gonorrhœa first shows itself as a discharge from the sex organs." "Professional prostitutes are not the only source of infection." The last sentence was cut out completely, and the other two were re-worded in order to avoid any reference to the sex organs. The result was much misery, doubt and misapprehension. Large numbers of people all over the country with ulcers or sores on any part of the body, afraid that they may be infected with V.D., wrote to the Ministry of Health for advice.

The Lancet had this comment to make: "This is the second occasion on which prudery has been allowed to hinder health education: it will be recalled that about a year ago advice to the public about washing the hands after evacuation of the bowel had to be withdrawn because the papers could not bring themselves to print *water closet*."

That battle has now been won. It is not surprising that when the facts of the matter were presented to the British public clearly and honestly, they took the necessary action and helped reduce the disease to a minimum.

But we have not even made a start towards finding the solution to the problem of homosexuality within our society. It is difficult to get anyone to admit that the problem exists. Most people prefer to shelter behind the cliché which runs: Life may be sordid but why call attention to it when there are so many more agreeable things in the world.

This problem exists whether we want it to or not, regardless of how society in general may shut its eyes to its reality. It cannot be argued that a topic such as this does not concern the clean-living normal man. The consequences of homosexuality are so widespread that the problem must be of first-rank importance to anyone who makes any pretence of serious thinking about social problems. It is not altogether an individual problem as is too largely assumed, for it has far reaching sociological implications.

It is significant that those who are most repulsed by the whole subject of homosexuality, and therefore should be the most anxious to prevent it, or at least reduce it to a minimum, are the very people who retreat behind a veil of silence on this vital issue. Yet we can make no progress towards prevention or reduction

22

unless we first try to understand it. We must start by admitting frankly that the problem exists, that it is of outstanding importance and that as yet no solution has been found to combat it. Only after we have discussed it and brought the whole subject into the light, can we hope to make any progress towards a solution.

This book will attempt to face the social problems connected with homosexuality no matter how unsavoury the facts may be. It is important to realize at the outset that homosexuality is not a separate entity but a question of degree. Although there are a few exclusive and complete homosexuals for whom heterosexual relations would be impossible and unthinkable, over the population as a whole there is an imperceptible gradation from wholly homosexual to wholly heterosexual. A man may be completely heterosexual or completely homosexual, but the great majority of men come somewhere in between these two extremes. It follows that homosexual activities may be followed by men who are not exclusively homosexual, but who have homosexual tendencies. These tendencies may be strong or weak depending on many factors. A strict definition of a homosexual might include only those who are exclusively homosexual, but for the sake of convenience the word "homosexual" in this book will include all those who have strong tendencies towards this abnormality.

A further definition is necessary to avoid another popular misconception. In this book, homosexuality refers to an attitude of mind in which the affections are turned towards a member of the same sex. This need not include specific overt sexuality although, of course, it is often implied. In this sense, homosexuality arouses the same emotions and desires as in heterosexuality in which the affections are turned towards members of the opposite sex. It therefore includes sexual activities or reactions between two adult men. It does *not* include infantile and early pubertal homosexuality which can be regarded as part of the normal development of a child. And it does *not* include the pseudo-homosexuals or the infanto-homosexuals, two classes of perversion which the layman is apt to confuse with true homosexuality.

The pseudo-homosexual is the man with heterosexual inclinations who indulges in homosexual intercourse as a substitution. Nearly all pseudo-homosexuals are of sub-normal intelligence; many of them are feeble-minded. This abnormality usually comes into one of three categories: (1) The men with low intelligence who would prefer a female partner but who find it easier to commit sodomy with other men. (2) The sub-normal who have confused ideas about sex and in order to avoid

23

"getting a girl into trouble" or catching V.D., they will commit sodomy with another man. (3) There are some men who will accept any kind of sexual relations wherever and as often as it can be found. They are also probably sub-normal and are only concerned with the gratification of their lust. Their behaviour is epitomized in the Asiatic saying: "A girl for a boy, a boy for a man, and a goat for sheer delight."

The infanto-homosexuals are attracted to young boys. It is a much more complicated perversion because not only is the sexual impulse diverted to the same sex, but also all the normal associations of a sexual attraction are sacrificed. The infanto-homosexuals can expect to find no sympathy or companionship in the boys they seek. They are often of the same mental age as the children they try to seduce. It may be caused by a repressed homosexual impulse which breaks out in later life as a regression to the pervert's own childhood. Sometimes they are equally attracted to young girls.

The genuine homosexual turns towards adults of his own sex as naturally as a normal man is sexually attracted by a woman as a potential mate and he is no more attracted to a young boy than a heterosexual is attracted to a young girl. In spite of popular ideas to the contrary, it is rare to find a man who is greatly attracted to both men and boys.

Confusion is sometimes caused by the word *homosexual*. It is often thought that this only refers to sexual relations between men, but the word *homo* comes not from the Latin, but from the Greek (meaning *sameness*). It therefore refers to any sexual activity between members of the same sex.

On the whole there seems to be a much greater tolerance of Lesbianism than of homosexuality between men. Women are assumed to be more concerned with the affectional side of life and enjoy more liberties. They are allowed to be more expressive and intimate between themselves; for example, kissing between two women is completely accepted as a natural mode of expression of affection. Women are less suspect if they live together than are men; this may have some connection with the common idea that men are sexually more active than are women. Indeed, there is a vague and unspoken idea among some people that two women who indulge in a certain amount of sex play are doing no more than day-dreaming until the right man comes along. The social implications of Lesbianism differ in many ways from the problems of homosexuality between men and no attempt can be made to deal with them in this book.

Male homosexuality may run the whole gamut from ardent sensuality to spiritual love, but it is essentially between two men who know what they are doing and who, in spite of all the pressures of society, find that they can only be sexually stimulated by certain members of their own sex. In the next chapter we shall find that the number who are affected in this way is far larger than is generally realized.

An evaluation of the effects of this abnormality is worthwhile not only from the point of view of the individual sufferers, but also for the additional knowledge which it will give of psychoneurotic distortions. The mind cannot be divided into a series of separate compartments and an emotional disturbance will influence all the actions and attitudes of a man. As there are many thousands of homosexuals in this country alone, it can be seen that the social aspects of the problem are very important.

CHAPTER II

PREVALENCE

Thousands of pounds are spent each year on cancer and T.B. research. This, of course, is right and proper and the money is well spent. Yet it is doubtful whether the suffering caused by both these diseases combined is anything like as great as the suffering caused by homosexuality. Many hundreds of pounds are given to animal-care societies while scores of hundreds are left to suffer from this disease.

It will be argued that homosexuality cannot be considered in the same light; it is a degeneration of the human functions, a perversion. In the Journal of Criminal Psychopathology, Karpman[43] has this to say about homosexuality:

"By stigmatizing the condition [homosexuality] as a perversion one does not solve the problem, but merely gives vent to a sense of moral indignation. These patients should be regarded neither as perverts nor as degenerates, but as sick persons whose sickness is derived from environmental sources on the basis of arrested development in the biologic and psychic evolution of man. They are no more responsible for that than a patient is responsible for having a particular disease."

A more enlightened protest against large scale research into homosexuality will run like this: Granted that these people are not entirely to blame for their condition, we cannot spend time and money on a few deviants from the normal life. Every society has its misfits; we cannot turn the world upside down to accommodate them.

But are they misfits? If by misfits we mean those individuals who make trouble for their society, they are not. If we include all those who find no congenial outlet for their sexual drive, then they may be called misfits, but they make up a not inconsiderable proportion of the total population. And this will include many well known and useful members of the community. This was noted by Ivan Bloch[7] many years ago:

"Men of the highest and most respected professions—above all, judges, practising physicians, men of science, theologians and scholars—have described themselves to me as having been through and through homosexuals from early childhood."

It may well be that there is no other emotional problem that effects so many people. Unfortunately one of the results of this conspiracy of silence and lack of research is that there are no reliable figures on the prevalence of homosexuality.

Such official records as exist are of little scientific value: they merely record the number of charges and convictions. Even if we were to add the number of suspects known to the police, we would still have no accurate measure of the problem, but there can be little doubt that it is considerable.

One of the first to try to find the incidence of homosexuality was a German, Magnus Hirschfeld. He became interested in the problem half a century ago when a young man who was his patient killed himself on the eve of his marriage rather than enter upon a sexual relationship which his homosexuality led him to dread. This is by no means a unique case and many more put off their marriage by some less drastic method for exactly the same reason.

Dr. Hirschfeld persuaded 10,000 men and women to fill out a questionnaire containing 130 questions. From this information he estimated that in the Germany of his day with a population of sixty million, nearly a million and a half men and women had inclinations which were largely or completely homosexual.

Since then various psychologists have made estimates from their clinical observations. Unfortunately these are far from accurate because by far the largest number of homosexuals never consult a psychiatrist. Others visit a psychiatrist for some other reason and are so frightened of social stigma that they have not dared to admit their homosexual tendencies to the local doctor, and sometimes not even to the psychiatrist until the treatment has been under way for some time. There is also a financial factor here. Unless a man is ordered to have a compulsory treatment by the Court, few people can afford to pay for prolonged analysis. Many homosexuals manage to avoid conflict with the law and few can afford psychiatric treatment.

Consequently the figures advanced by the clinical psychologists take into account only the extreme cases. Until the Kinsey Report was published, it was not understood to what extent homosexuality was to be found in people living an apparently normal life on the surface.

Sexual Behaviour in the Human Male, by Kinsey, Pomeroy and Martin, is based upon data obtained from 5,300 Americans carefully selected and balanced to give a faithful picture of American male sexual behaviour. Parts of the information were based on as many as 12,000 cases. When the series of nine books

27

is complete, Kinsey and his associates will have interviewed over 100,000 men and women.

Public opinion polls have become an exact science in America, but Kinsey's detailed and thorough methods, involving a personal interview with each person and a code to insure absolute secrecy, demand even greater respect. The very large numbers dealt with and the careful training given to each investigator make the results worth the most careful study.

The most startling fact to emerge from the Kinsey Report is that 37 per cent. of the male population has had some homosexual experience between the beginning of adolescence and old age. As Kinsey himself writes:[45]

"In brief, homosexuality is not the rare phenomenon which it is ordinarily considered to be but a type of behaviour which ultimately may involve as much as half the male population."

Of the men who are still unmarried by the time they are 35 years old, over 50 per cent. have had homosexual experience. Kinsey remarks that his associates and himself were quite unprepared to find this high incidence. They were assailed with doubts and felt that somehow they had stumbled upon an unusual segment of the population. It was only after they had taken many other samples, compared them with each other and cross-checked in twelve different ways that they felt certain that their figures were well founded. He concludes:

"There can be no question that the actual incidence of the homosexual is at least 37 and 50 per cent. as given above. The tests show that the actual frequency may be as much as 5 per cent. higher, or even higher."

Thus more than one man in three has had some experience of homosexuality and of the unmarried men, over half have been involved in such behaviour. Kinsey's investigation showed that the frequency of overt homosexuality was much higher than had ever been realized at every social level, in every age group, in every walk of life, in town and country, in single and married men.

He reports that 10 per cent. of the married men between the ages of 21-25 have indulged in homosexuality. The incidence decreased in the older married men (6·8 per cent. in 26-30, 4·8 per cent. in 31-35) but Kinsey believes that the true incidence is much higher than they were able to record. Married men with a social position to maintain are reluctant to contribute their sex histories to a research study. It is probable that a good many married men who were having homosexual relations would deliberately avoid contributing their histories to this investigation. Kinsey found hundreds of younger individuals in his case histories who reported homosexual contacts with these older, socially established, married men.

It is to be expected that the incidence among single males would be much higher. In fact, Kinsey found that the incidence increased with age: 27·5 per cent. of single males at the age 21-25 are having homosexual experiences. At the 26-30 age group it was 35·8 per cent., while at 36-40 it was 38·7 per cent. Of the men who had been married but were now widowed or divorced, 17·6 per cent. of the 26-30 age group had post-marital homosexual intercourse, and 6·2 per cent. of the 36-40 age group.

In the entire male population of all ages, about 30 per cent. have been brought to climax at least once in mouth-genital relations with other males, and 14 per cent. had brought other males to climax by the same techniques.

Kinsey divided his histories into three educational groups. He found that of men who left school after grade school 6·9 per cent. used homosexual outlets before they were 20, 10·8 per cent. of the high school men used homosexual outlets before they were 20, and 2·4 per cent. of the men who went on to college. He notes that although the high school men condemned, ridiculed and punished homosexuality more than the other two groups, their rate of activity was highest.

It should be noted that these figures include only those people who have had physical contact with other males, and who were brought to orgasm as a result of such contacts. It does not include the large number of people who respond to homosexual stimulation and who have had some homosexual contact although it has not led to orgasm. It also leaves out another large group who are erotically aroused by a homosexual stimulus but, for various reasons, have repressed or diverted their sexual drive. Many of these men have homosexual relations in fantasy but not in practice.

Kinsey's records show a wide variety of types of homosexual behaviour. Individuals run the whole gamut from one experience to thousands. In an attempt to get over this difficulty, he arranged the histories in seven different grades, from exclusively heterosexual to exclusively homosexual with five intermediate grades. This grading depended not only upon the actual overt experiences of the subject, but also upon his fantasies, inclinations and psychosexual reactions. From these classifications he was able to find the following results:

37 per cent. of the total male population has at least some overt homosexual experience to the point of orgasm between adolescence and old age. In addition, 13 per cent. react

29

erotically to other males without having overt homosexual contacts after the onset of adolescence. So 50 per cent. react erotically with or without overt experience.

25 per cent. have more than incidental homosexual experience or reactions in their histories for at least three years between the ages of 16 and 55. Passing experiences have been eliminated from the data by showing only ratings that have involved a period of at least three years after the males turn 16.

18 per cent. have at least as much of the homosexual as the heterosexual in their histories for at least three years between the ages of 16 and 55.

13 per cent. have more homosexual than heterosexual experiences and reactions in their histories for at least three years between the ages of 16 and 55.

10 per cent. are more or less exclusively homosexual in their experiences and reactions for at least three years between the ages of 16 and 55.

8 per cent. are exclusively homosexual for at least three years between the ages of 16 and 55.

4 per cent. are exclusively homosexual throughout their lives.

In other words, over a tenth part of the male population are more or less homosexual for a number of years and one in every thirteen men are completely homosexual for a period of their lives. One in twenty-five do not have any normal sexual experience or reactions.

All of Kinsey's information was obtained inside the United States. It is the only thorough and complete investigation into sexual behaviour in the world. But the findings can only be applied to this country with the utmost caution. Kinsey has pointed out some of the variations from area to area within the United States. We should expect to find other variations in this country.

Nevertheless the Kinsey results have shown that we must re-adjust our attitude to homosexuality. Until a British Kinsey appears on the scene, we must assume that this problem is one that affects every corner of our island and is not just a series of isolated incidents as some judges, clergymen, doctors and educators would have us believe.

Indeed it is possible that the incidence of homosexuality is higher in this country than in the United States. More than one American visitor has said that the problem seems more acute over here than in their own country. One American homosexual has settled over here because, in his own words, "it is easier to find a partner, sometimes from among those who are so high-hat about it."

Only recently one prominent Swedish business-man shocked the reporters by stating that the biggest surprise of his visit to England was the number of homosexuals to be seen around London. Similar comments have been made by Frenchmen who are supposed to be so enlightened on sex matters; in point of fact this enlightenment is confined to the outward technique and elegance of their sex play.

It would not be so surprising if a scientific investigation revealed that the incidence of homosexuality was even greater than Kinsey found in the United States. The unnatural restraint and prudishness of parts of our sex code might well be a source of a great deal of abnormality. Alec Waugh, Bruce Marshall and others have drawn attention to the dangers of frustrated sexual impulses in our all-male public schools. The intense cultivation of games in England has an echo in the Athenians' worship of the male human body.

Various other estimates of the incidence of homosexuality have been made in this country. In the main they seem to vary between 2 per cent. and 8 per cent. Most of the lower figures were reported before Kinsey drew attention to the universality of the problem. Even if we take the figure of 4 per cent. which on the available evidence seems to be a very conservative estimate, this means that there are over 650,000 homosexuals in England and Wales alone. One out of twenty-five of the men in this country are completely homosexual. In addition there are at least another two million (13 per cent.) with strong homosexual tendencies.*

To those who protest that such a thing is absurd, let it be remembered that a common error is to imagine that all homosexuals look like "Nancy boys". By far the largest number of homosexuals cannot be distinguished from the normal heterosexual either in physique or in intelligence. In spite of the similarity of build, some homosexuals can be recognized immediately by their clothes, their walk, their voices or effeminate manners. But these also are strictly in the minority. Most of the homosexuals are desperately anxious to cover up their abnormality, even if this means joining in the general chorus of contempt for other homosexuals in order to keep in with the accepted code of society.

There can now be little doubt that it is a problem of large

* The Registrar-General's *Statistical Review of England and Wales* for the year 1948 reports that there are 16,331,000 males in England over the age of 15.

31

proportions. It can no longer be regarded as a few isolated examples of Nature's throw-backs. Man is infinitely variable and every generation can be expected to produce its quota of cranks. Perhaps it is just as well that it does. But the homosexuals cannot be put in this category because the numbers are far too large. In spite of the absence of accurate statistics for this country, it is clear from the existing information that:

(1) The majority of males pass through a homosexual stage at one period of their lives.

(2) A large number of people who now enjoy heterosexual relations have had some homosexual experience.

(3) A not inconsiderable minority who are attempting to lead normal, socially approved lives have homosexual difficulties.

(4) A much larger proportion than has hitherto been realized, are exclusively homosexual.

THE CAUSES OF HOMOSEXUALITY

CHAPTER III

CONGENITAL

Each homosexual is an individual unto himself. He has his own family background and his own personal history. Very few general statements can be made about the cause and cure of homosexuality. The surroundings and experience of each person differ so widely that any number of things might be the cause of the emotional conflict that sets up a personality disorder.

An attempt will be made in this section to list the main causes of homosexuality. Although it is divided into four parts bringing together one congenital and three environmental influences, it is important to realize that these parts are in no sense independent of one another. Most psychologists now agree that there are a number of different factors which tend to create a homosexual pattern and homosexual practices are nearly always the result of two or more of these factors.

Many research workers have been impressed by the fact that homosexuality has appeared in every age and in every civilization. The attitudes of various communities towards homosexuality has varied from complete tolerance to savage persecution. But no matter what the reactions have been, it has always been irrepressible and no civilization has succeeded in stamping it out. This has led many psychologists to suppose that there must be a strong hereditary factor in the development of homosexuality.

Lange[49] in his investigation of identical twins found that one pair were separated at birth and reared in very different surroundings, but both showed homosexual tendencies. Others have claimed to have found some evidence that homosexuality recurs in some families in circumstances in which propinquity or common environment were unlikely to be the causative factor.

Sir Norwood East and W. H. Hubert in their report on the *Psychological Treatment of Crime*[17] suggests that homosexuality is so often mixed with other neuroses and perversions that environmental factors alone could not produce so frequently so complicated a pattern. Their studies, however, were restricted to persons convicted of a homosexual offence or other prison inmates. It is doubtful if all homosexuals would have so many emotional disturbances.

35

Hirschfeld developed a more interesting theory which underlined the personality factor. He maintained that homosexuals were intergrades and belonged to what he called "The Third Sex". These people, both men and women, were neither completely masculine nor completely feminine, but somewhere in between. Weininger[75] went still further and suggested that we all had a measure of physical intersexuality in our make up. As long ago as 1904 he wrote:

"There is no absolutely male and no absolutely female individual; in every man there is something of woman, and in every woman something of man, and that between the two various transitional forms, sexual *intermediate stages* exist."

Theo Lang[48] made an interesting investigation in 1940. He started with the hypothesis that if male homosexuals were intergrades, then it is possible that they were really females in male bodies. In other words these men were genetically female. Now in any large number of people, it has been established that for every 100 girls born, there are 106 boys. This ratio of 106 males to 100 females has been statistically tested many times and must be accepted. But if it is true that a proportion of male homosexuals are actually transformed females, then this would upset the 106:100 ratio. In fact, one must expect to find a larger number of males among the brothers and sisters of male homosexuals because, according to Lang, some of them are not males but females disguised as males. In his own words: "We must expect more than 106 males for 100 females, since a series of genotypical females would be hidden among the phenotypical male probands."

He went into the detailed family history of 1,015 male homosexuals and found that they had 1,734 brothers and 1,432 sisters. This gives a ratio of 121:100 which deviates clearly from the normal proportion of 106:100. Taking only those cases who were over 25, and so were more likely to represent exclusive homosexuals, he found that the ratio was 128:100. He suggested that these results indicated that many cases of homosexuality are hereditarily determined and are best explained by a genetic mechanism.

Some homosexuals appear to have semi-female bodies and various studies of the bodily structure have been made to try to establish whether this intergrade theory is true. Henry[34] studied thirty-three homosexual mental patients. He concluded that the homosexual male is characterized by a feminine carrying angle of the arm, long legs, narrow hips, large muscles, deficient hair on the face, chest and back, feminine distribution of pubic hair, a high-pitched voice and a small penis and testicles.

This description seems to line up with the popular conception of a "pansy". Certainly it is possible to grade human groups in such a way that between the most masculine and the most feminine, there will be others who seem to fall in the middle. This is true whether one uses the popular standards such as depth of voice, male or female mannerisms, growth of beard and type of hair, etc., or whether one uses more accurate measurements such as size of breasts, pelvic measurements, hip-shoulder proportions, etc.

There is no doubt that such grades exist. But there is still considerable doubt whether there is a positive correlation between these grades and homosexuality. It is not disputed that some homosexuals are effeminate, but this theory does not account for the much larger number of homosexuals who have thoroughly masculine bodies. Quite often the homosexual who appears effeminate in speech, walk and talk is found to have a masculine physique which he disguises because he wants to look feminine. The presence of feminine characteristics may be no more than outward evidence that the individual has been brought up in a very feminine environment. The male prostitutes who go out of their way to look effeminate in order to attract trade are, for the most part, heterosexual out of business hours.

There are also quite a large number of men with striking secondary sexual physical characteristics belonging to the female and even sometimes with various degrees of hermaphroditism, who are without demonstrable homosexual tendencies. Wortis[78] and many others concluded that convincing evidence for any constant or typical intersexual traits among male homosexuals is still wanting. It is a popular misconception to assume that a man with certain feminine characteristics is sure to be a homosexual. It may well be that many such men do have homosexual experience because society drives them to it by expecting it of them and forcing them into an environment where homosexual opportunities are plentiful.

Although information about the outward physical characteristics is confused, the recent advances made in endocrinology have opened a new field of research. For a long time it has seemed as if disturbances of the sex glands have played an important role in various neuro-psychiatric conditions. A neurosis often results in the impairment of the menstrual function in females and in loss of potency in males. Many investigators have sought to find a connection between hormone excretion and homosexuality.

Glass, Devel and Wright[30] state that in homosexuality the ratio of male and female hormones is disproportionate. Neustadt and Myerson[58] examined twenty-nine homosexuals for hormone excretion and found that in twenty-five the male hormone was relatively low and the female hormone relatively high. This was not solely correlated to the physical build, but primarily to their overt homosexual conduct and feelings. One case showed a "high normal" amount of male hormones, and low female hormone excretion; investigation of his history revealed that he was, in reality, a rapist who practised sodomy and was indiscriminate in his sexual drive. He represented the only case of sodomy in the entire series. As these signs (high female, low male hormone excretion) were not discovered in other sexual abnormalities, it may lead to a way of finding which are true homosexuals.

Williams[77] found a biological difference between feminine-type homosexuals (who had passive anal or active oral experiences) and masculine-type homosexuals (who had active anal or passive oral experiences). On the other hand, castration does not increase a man's tendency towards homosexuality, nor does the injection of female hormones. The administration of male hormones to an effeminate man will increase the sexual drive but will not alter the choice of his sexual partner.

There are many other similar investigations but, at the moment, there is no practical aspect in considering homosexuality from the standpoint of a biological defect or of misdirected hormone activity. Such research is, of course, essential for the medical men before they can hope to find a satisfactory cure. For our purposes we can only note that malfunction of the glands may be one of the factors that cause sexual deviation. It is, however, unlikely to be the major cause in many cases and in the majority of cases, the psychological and environmental influences are more important.

CHAPTER IV

EARLY INFLUENCES

SOME CLINICAL WORKERS report that they can find no difference between the physique of the homosexual and heterosexual, either in physical measurements or by biochemical and endocrine tests. Therefore they believe that the causes of homosexuality are wholly environmental. Even those who maintain that there is some congenital influence agree that the most important causes are to be found in the childhood experiences of the man.

Freud discovered that the sexual impulses exist from birth. During the first five years of life the sex instincts are directed towards external objects. A child brought up in an institution, or in other unusual circumstances, will have a modified experience, but the average child will direct his sexual impulses towards persons within the family circle.

These sexual impulses pass through various stages, starting with the breast-feeding stage where the erotic zone is the mouth. Later when the child is being taught to be clean and to control his elimination, the erotic zone is the anus. At another stage the genitals become the main zone and, later still, the Œdipus situation arises when the child requires the mother's love and seeks to compete with the father. Each of these stages contain powerful sex urges aiming at gratification. This is quite normal in a child, but when these impulses are found in an adult, they are branded as sexual perversions.

These familial sexual impulses meet with resistance and all instincts that meet with emotional conflicts tend to be repressed. Therefore the largest part of infantile sexuality remains unconscious. From about five until puberty a sexual latency period exists, during which, in the majority of instances, these earlier infantile impulses disappear completely. But any number of difficulties or accidents can cause a regression to one of these stages. When this happens in an adult, this regression of the sex drive to an early infantile stage will result in abnormal sexual behaviour of one kind or another.

Homosexuality, in common with most other sexual deviations,

is derived and built up from infantile sexual drives. They are part of the normal sex impulses of a child and only become abnormal when they appear in adult behaviour as a regression to an earlier stage.

Only the main principles of the Freudian theory have been stated here. Any observant mother whose mind is not clouded with prudery could confirm most of the points by watching her child at play. The elaborations made by later disciples of Freud cannot be recognized so easily.

For example, Fenichel[21] maintains that homosexuality is often caused by a disappointment in later life which connects up with a deep-seated disappointment repressed from childhood. Fenichel explains this as a castration complex: "The patient is so insistent on a penis, he refuses to use it in his sexual partner—or he is unconsciously frightened of being without a penis, he rejects all sexual relations—or the female genitalis is perceived as an instrument of castration, an instrument which might bite off or tear the penis."

But such an elaboration cannot be substantiated and must, for the time being at least, remain in the realm of conjecture. It is more important to see how the basic principles apply in practice, to bring the rather abstruse psychological generalities nearer home into the family circle.

If anything happens to disturb the infant's love for his mother, this can be the cause of homosexual tendencies. In the normal course of events, the boy will be able to transfer the love for the mother to some other female. But if the boy is brought up in an institution with no mother substitute, or if the mother for some reason shows indifference or hostility to the boy, then he may not have learnt to love a woman, and so he will not be able to transfer his love to a female mate.

Conversely, if the mother monopolizes the boy and the father becomes unimportant and insignificant in the boy's life, then the feminine influence in the boy's environment may become too powerful. This is especially true if the mother is a widow, or the father is away from the home. The boy has no one to mould himself on and so identifies himself with the mother. This identification will include both the mother and her sexual position, so that he puts himself in the same position as the mother and can only love other males.

A third family complication which will make for homosexual tendencies is an aggressive father. If the father ill-treats the mother, is alcoholic or hostile, the boy will turn to the mother and come to rely upon her so much that the transfer to other females will be inhibited by an unconscious feeling of incest.

40

Yet another difficulty can occur during the stage when the erotic zone is being transferred from the anus to the genitals. If the child is made to understand that the business of elimination is rather disgusting and altogether unpleasant, this association may be transferred to the genitals. Eventually the boy's natural sexual impulses appear to him to be unpleasant and shameful and so he seeks another method of sexual expression which, to his unconscious self, does not have this strong association with shame. When too great an emphasis has been put on the control of elimination, there may be a tendency towards sodomy because the association between the anus and the genitals is still strong.

Any of these difficulties in the family circle can cause homosexual tendencies. These are influences that occur in the early stages. From the age of five, the infantile sexual drives are weaker, but there are still home influences that can mar the rest of a man's emotional life.

The mother who, desiring a girl, brings up her boy as girlishly as possible, cuts his hair like a girl's or dresses him in feminine clothes, can so influence her son's outlook that he will tend to think and act like a girl in matters of sex. If a girl is wanted and a boy arrives, the parents may unconsciously influence the child's development even when the mother does not go to such extremes. The child senses the wishes of the parents even though nothing is said. When he indulges in rough play which might be only natural for a boy, he is told that he is naughty. When he looks after his dolls or behaves like a girl in some other way, the parents are pleased. His habitual conduct is likely to be that which elicits greatest praise or distinction. To the extent that his interests, attitude and behaviour are out of harmony with his actual sex he is likely to meet circumstances which will accentuate his homosexual tendencies.

On the other hand, mothers and, more especially, fathers can put too great an emphasis on masculine pursuits. The proud father may be anxious that his son should excel in the rougher type of games and display all the he-man characteristics, when in fact the son is physically weaker than most of his companions. If the necessity of masculine pursuits is impressed upon the boy too forcibly, it may drive him to take refuge in explicit femininity.

Quite early in life the young boy comes across sex differentiations set up and accepted by society which can cause considerable difficulties if his inclinations and abilities run against the existing patterns. Some occupations are considered unmanly, some hobbies are reserved exclusively for women, some qualities (fastidiousness, sensitivity, neatness) are considered desirable in women but not in men. Our society has decreed that certain gifts and talents should occur only in females, but Nature often arranges a more even distribution.

Devereux in his study of the American Mohave Indians showed how this influence worked in a primitive society. The Indian fathers valued courage in battle above all other qualities and watched their little boys with such desperate intensity that a fair number of them, realizing that they could not fit into the men's society, gave up the struggle and assumed women's dress. In the same way our own society sometimes drives our boys to clothe their minds in women's dress.

In all this, it will be observed that a straightforward, unprejudiced, secure family life is the finest insurance against the development of homosexual tendencies. Friction between parents is so common that it would be a mistake to assume that it leads to homosexuality in their children. Nevertheless a large number of homosexuals come from maladjusted parents and broken homes. Under ideal circumstances the father should be an understanding, tolerant but virile and decisive male. The mother should have the gentleness, patience and passivity usually associated with womanhood. Any mixture such as an effeminate father and an aggressive, masculine mother is likely to be disconcerting to the child and lead to abnormalities in his sexual outlook.

These same qualities are equally important during adolescence when the boy's sexual impulses are reawakening. At this stage the boy must learn to transfer the love for his mother to some other female. This transfer can be hindered by social and religious movements in which close association between members of the same sex is encouraged, while meetings between boys and girls are viewed with suspicion.

Finally the boy's whole attitude to sex will depend largely upon his early influences. The parents must assume responsibility for the development of a healthy outlook, just as they are responsible for the development of other personality characteristics.

The sex code laid down by Western civilization can itself act as a barrier to the development of normal heterosexual impulses. When the whole business of sex is shrouded in shame and mystery, the boy may easily adopt sexual attitudes and preferences which will develop into homosexuality. Dr. Isaac Frost[28] has said: "Society has to take the blame for most sexual misbehaviour because society has kept people ignorant on sex matters. In my view, the most effective cause of sexual difficulty has been just plain ignorance."

Most doctors have been impressed by the "miraculous cures" that have been effected merely by telling the patient the facts of life. The more society obscures the fundamental sex issues with prudery, the more difficult it will be for the boy to learn the natural functions of reproduction.

CHAPTER V

SEDUCTION

THE RECORDS OF psychiatrists show that over 90 per cent. of the homosexual cases start by seduction. Often the first experience of ejaculation comes with an association with another boy or a man. Some investigators have come to the conclusion that this is the main cause of homosexuality. If this is true, it becomes a matter of supreme importance in connection with the social aspects as well as the causative factors.

The greatest danger of seduction is that it may alter the mental disposition of the boy. After having some sexual experience with another male, he may use this experience to build up powerful sexual fantasies. For example, he may imagine that he is with another male while masturbating and with frequent repetition, this may drive out heterosexual activities.

There are some authorities who go so far as to suggest that there is a physical common denominator in homosexuals, not due to any congenital characteristics, but because the more attractive and good-looking boys are more likely to be the focus of attention of older homosexuals. One would then expect to find that most of the good-looking males in the community had homosexual tendencies while few, if any, of the less attractive ones would have this predisposition. This proposition does not stand up to close examination, for it is obvious that there are thousands of good-looking young men who enjoy normal heterosexual relations and among the homosexuals, there are many who can make little claim to good looks or attractive features. This theory, like so many, has been founded on the popular assumption that all homosexuals look like "pansies" and can easily be recognized. In fact, by far the largest majority of homosexuals are microscopically indistinguishable from the other men in the community.

Although there is little doubt that the first experience can be an important stage in the life of a homosexual, it is important not to over emphasize the effects of an early seduction in an ordinary man. In fact, some people develop so strong a homosexual tendency early in life that a seduction can be regarded as merely the final stage in what would be the inevitable result. The following two cases histories illustrate this point:

Case I. K—— was 16 years old when he met a man who seduced him. Here is part of his story: "He smiled at me as I left the bus stop and so I turned back. I thought that I knew him or, rather, that I was supposed to know him. We talked for a time and then he took me to the pictures where he put his hand on my thighs. I remember being surprised, but I was more surprised that this should happen in the cinema than by what he did. After a short time, he suggested that we should go for a walk. This was the first time that I had ever left a cinema without seeing the film right through, but I was quite willing. We went into a field where we both got partially undressed. After a certain amount of play on the ground, I turned over with my back to him. I cannot explain now why I did this except that at the time it seemed the natural thing to do. Although the man did eventually commit sodomy,* I remember he was surprised at my haste and told me not to let everyone do that to me. . . . I can honestly say that I did not know that such a thing was possible until it happened."

Case II. L—— was an ex-choir boy and Boy Scout of 15 who had had no sexual experience until he met an older boy in a crowd watching a street entertainer. ". . . He quietly put his hand in my pocket and played with me. I was frightened by this and moved away. He followed me and I waited for him. He suggested that we go to a public lavatory. I hesitated but eventually agreed to go if he promised not to touch me. When we were inside the lavatory with the door locked, I felt strangely excited and important. I told him to take his clothes off. He protested that this was dangerous, but I insisted that he remove every single bit of his clothing. I then admired his body, but when I touched it I felt I could no longer control myself and rushed out the door. I intended to run away, but when I got to the entrance of the public lavatory, I waited for him and when he came out, we went for a walk. When we came to a deserted building, I suggested that we go in. This time we both undressed and indulged in mutual masturbation.* This was the first time I had ever done anything with a man, and yet from the start I felt as if I should do the leading. It made me feel important and powerful."

These two cases may be classified as seductions by older and

---

* In these and the following cases, the actual words of the subject have been modified.

more experienced homosexuals, but there seems little doubt that in these, and many other cases, the tendency was already firmly planted. It is reasonable to suppose that this tendency can be so strong in some people that sooner or later some factor in the subject's environment will release this homosexual influence and convert it into overt activity. The next two cases show this same strong tendency in older people.

Case III. T—— was 19 years old and in the Army when he went out with a friend and spent about an hour in a bar. "We were both a bit drunk and on the way back we were fighting and playing around. In the middle of all this I put my arm around him and kissed him. I had never done this before to any man although I have always been interested in men and have dreamed about them many times. When I found that he did not object, the kisses became more passionate and we held each other very tight and felt each other all over until we both had an orgasm. The next evening I suggested that we do the same thing again, but my friend was very angry. He said that he had been too drunk to know what he was doing and that I had taken an unfair advantage of him. He avoided me as much as possible in the future and he used to call me queer. But for me, the whole episode was a release. I had discovered that it was possible to get a feeling that I had never experienced when I had kissed a girl."

Case IV. E—— is now a successful architect of 28 years who has been married for five years and has a small daughter. "At school I was very attracted to a boy of my own age, and I had day-dreams in which I imagined that we were masturbating each other. When I was about twenty, I began to get disturbed about the way my thoughts always seemed to be about men. I read a few books on sex and got the idea that it was because I was unmarried and was not having any sex. Then I met M—— and felt that she would make a good wife although I can't say I ever felt any physical desire for her at any time. I was sure everything would be all right after we were married, but the first few weeks of attempted intercourse were terrible. At the time I thought our consistent failures were because it was the first time either of us had any sex with a partner. After a time I discovered that I could do much better and begin to satisfy my wife when I arranged to have intercourse in the dark so that I could imagine that I was with another man. I still do this and unless I concentrate all my imagination upon one man or another, I cannot come to a climax. I used to go out and look for attractive men so that they could become the object of my fantasy when I got back home. One day a man noticed me looking at him and came up to speak to me. We arranged to meet a few days later. Of course by this time I knew what to expect and since then I have been having sex with him and other men. My wife does not know about this and for the sake of my daughter, I do not want her to find out, but I suppose it will all blow up one day."

These two cases show strong homosexual tendencies but neither of them found overt experience until relatively late in life. In the second case, the result of this will probably be that three lives will be scarred instead of one.

The seduction may be the turning-point in a number of histories, but if the homosexual tendency is strong enough, it will eventually come out in some form or other. On the other hand there is strong evidence to show that the boy with only weak homosexual tendencies will survive a seduction without disability. Rosanoff[64] writes, "seduction can only be of lasting effect if its direction corresponds with the inherent tendencies of the subject".

Doshay[14] found that, among 108 unselected cases who between the ages of 7 and 16 had been involved in sexual delinquencies, there was "not a single instance of a known sex violation in adult life." Doshay states that the most frequent sexual offence in the cases he investigated was sodomy with adult men, older and younger boys, or with girls; he observes that "these practices . . . ought not, when occurring among juveniles, to be regarded in too morbid a light, nor should the boys be considered 'perverts' or 'homosexuals' as noted in some of the texts. . . . Of 256 cases, only two . . . revealed such deep interest in and craving for homosexual practices as to warrant the description of 'homosexual'."

The findings were also confirmed by the very thorough investigations of Bender and Blau. Judges and magistrates often assume that the boy victim of a sex offence will suffer for the rest of his life from the mental wound inflicted at the same time. But children often escape any lasting mental injury because they do not attach as much importance to sex as adults.

The next two cases are unusual because they describe two very similar seductions on two boys who had two very different predispositions. These two boys were both of the same age and went to the same school where they were seduced by the same schoolmaster. Apparently this schoolmaster encouraged the boys to come up to his private study when they had difficulty with their French preparation. The first boy went up one day and

47

was seduced by this man who told him to come up again when he felt like it. Some years later he recalled the episode.

Case V. "When I left the man's study, I felt awful and was quite certain that I would never go up to his study again. But I did, about twice a week over a period of four months. Of course I was only 14 at the time and I got the schoolboy idea into my head that he was hypnotizing me or casting some kind of spell over me that made me go up to his room. Each time I felt ashamed and disgusted after it was all over, but I didn't seem able to stop myself. Then he was caught in the act with some other boy, there was a big scandal and he left. When I look back at it now, I am disgusted by the fact that after the first occasion, it was me that provoked the man; I used to walk up into the trap. But it was just a passing phase. I suppose it could have happened to anyone."

Case VI. The other boy went up to this schoolmaster's study to seek some help with his French and was also seduced. He told a schoolboy friend what had happened and this friend informed him that he would go insane if he went on doing it. He continued: "I never went near that man for weeks on end until one day I got so stuck with my work that I just had to get some help. I was frightened when I entered the study, but when I left I was disappointed that nothing happened. Until then I had managed to put the first experience out of my mind, but within a few days of my second visit, I invented another excuse to go up to his study. We talked about the French but as he made no effort to do anything else, I touched his hand. He smiled and I believe he knew what was in my mind, but nothing happened. Not long after that I started having homosexual relations with another boy of my own age and lost interest in the man."

These two cases illustrate the seduction is unlikely to have any permanent effect unless the seeds of homosexuality have already been sown. One more case will show the effect of a seduction on a man who seems to have had very weak homosexual tendencies.

Case VII. This concerns a medical student who in a spirit of youthful indiscretion decided that he would understand how to deal with homosexuals only after he had had the necessary experience. "After enquiring from what I thought was a reliable source, I took up my station at one of the well-known meeting-places. After over an hour of waiting around, I began to get discouraged so I picked on a likely-looking man and followed him

48

around. When he became aware of the fact that he was being shadowed, he waited for me to catch up with him and then asked: 'Do I owe you some money?' I didn't find anyone that day, but I got a contact through someone else a few weeks later. I met this man on some quiet street corner and agreed to go back with him to his room. I won't say I was disgusted or revolted at what happened then, I was just plain bored and disinterested. The man indicated that he did not think much of me either. The whole experience must be written off as a failure and it certainly has not helped me to understand the homosexuals."

Except in the unusual circumstances of two younger boys experimenting together, almost any overt homosexual experience must start with an older, more experienced person. But it is not always easy to be sure which one is really the seducer. Often it has become clear that the so-called victim is the seducer and that the sexual act with the older boy or man has been actively sought as an expression of the younger boy's unconscious impulses and fantasies. Friedlander[27] writes: "More often than not, young boys will offer themselves, if not in words, then by gestures, to older men."

It is just possible that a man with homosexual tendencies will go through life without ever meeting a situation that will lead him to overt activities. Some men who appear to be leading heterosexual lives have confessed that they have had an unusual interest in men as long as they can remember. The first overt experience may be at any age, sometimes middle age or even later. When an old man of fifty or sixty is before the Court for a homosexual offence, he may declare that this is his very first overt act and there may be good reasons for believing this.

But this is exceptional. Most of the people who have developed homosexual tendencies due to early influences in their up-bringing will sooner or later meet the situation which will expose them to the risk of overt activity. In so far as this tendency is not a fixed quantity but varies from person to person, the results of seduction are important. It may be that when a person with only weak homosexual tendencies is exposed to frequent seduction, these tendencies become more powerful than they would have been otherwise.

But for the most part the influence has been exaggerated. For those with no predisposition towards homosexuality, it has only a temporary effect at the most. Kinsey's research suggests that over a third of the population were seduced, or at least initiated, into homosexual practices at one time or another. Many well-adjusted heterosexual adults will be able to recall homosexual

49

experiences amounting to seduction in their early history. Stanley-Jones[67] has suggested that the incidence of homosexual behaviour in some public schools is higher than 50 per cent. Most of these people have been able to develop normal heterosexual impulses at a later date.

CHAPTER VI

ALL-MALE ENVIRONMENT

ONE MORE CAUSE OF homosexuality remains to be considered. It has already been noted that there is a danger of impairing the heterosexual development of a boy if he is prevented from meeting and learning about the opposite sex. Various social and religious organizations and boarding schools have already been mentioned in this connection.

It is not always realized how tragic the consequences of the discovery of such practices can be to a young boy. Although he hardly knows what he is doing, he may be humiliated before the whole school and sent home in disgrace. This may leave a scar on his personality for the rest of his life; he may find himself ostracized and driven into the company of other homosexuals. Yet such harsh punishment is inflicted not on an isolated case, but on a chance discovery of what is known to be common practice in schools.

Sometimes this segregation from the female is so complete that it can have an effect upon adults who have previously developed heterosexual impulses. These circumstances are exceptional, but they occur sufficiently often in our Western civilization to make them a contributing cause.

The all-male environment in the Services, ships, monasteries, hostels for workmen in isolated places (foresters, builders, engineers) are examples of this. The experiences of prisoners of war in Germany and Japan are interesting because these camps contained men from every walk of life and of every conceivable temperament.

Case VIII. This history of one young prisoner of war will serve to illustrate how abnormal the situation can get. This man was a good-looking airman of 21 who was a practising homosexual before he was captured. With the same incredible ingenuity which other prisoners of war used for more praiseworthy ends, he made up a complete female attire for himself and even manufactured some exotic scent which he spread all over his body. He grew his hair long and walked and talked like a woman. His one object was to arouse erotic excitement in his fellow prisoners and he was extremely successful. Although food was very scarce he lived well and was never short of anything. The record of his daily sexual extravagances do him no credit, but the variety and number of his partners indicate that many of the prisoners of war were having overt homosexual experiences.

The histories of these prisoners can be classified into three stages. One group were having no homosexual contacts as far as was known. This group formed quite a small minority where the men had been imprisoned for two years or more. A second group consisted of those who were having secret "affairs", but owing to the lack of privacy in camps of this sort, the secret was usually discovered before very long. Many of this group were outwardly hostile to all forms of homosexuality until they were discovered. Then there were those who openly admitted having overt homo- sexual experiences and made advances to other prisoners. Long- term prisoners tended to pass through all three stages.

To many of these men in these prisoner of war camps, these homosexual stirrings were a new problem. The tendency was weak and had been repressed into the unconscious with ease; in the normal everyday life of these men, many of whom were married, these difficulties had not had an opportunity to come to the surface. Many of the men fought valiantly against these tendencies when they first appeared, but in the majority of cases, the all-male environment and the absence of normal sex life were too much for them.

From the point of view of society, a temporary deviation when the individual is denied the normal conditions of that society cannot be considered to be very important. But now we must consider whether the homosexual experiences of these men in camps, ships, hostels and other all-male communities will have any permanent effect. If they revert to normal behaviour as soon as the situation becomes normal, there is little to worry about. But if this homosexual influence is found to have a lasting effect it can become an important cause in the spread of homosexuality.

In this connection it is worth reporting the results of an experiment that Jenkins[42] carried out with rats. He discovered that if the rats were kept apart and the male rats had no oppor- tunity to contact the female rats, then after some time homo- sexual activities would begin. As the length of time that they were kept apart was increased, so the amount of homosexual behaviour increased. When this behaviour was well established he put back the females among the males but they showed little heterosexual interest and were not attracted to the females. The number of those which remained homosexual and the number of those that regained their heterosexuality was strictly dependent upon the length of time they had been kept away from the females. The longer the segregation the greater the number of rats which showed diminished heterosexuality on mixing with the females.

Any generalization of these results can only be applied to human animals with extreme caution. Nevertheless there are a number of cases where the individual has been unable to revert to heterosexual interests.

Case IX. D—— was a prisoner of war for over four years. He was an intelligent man, a research chemist in civilian life and an officer in the R.A.F. He had a brief homosexual experience at school but was not troubled by it later. He married before he joined the Service and enjoyed heterosexual relations. Fairly soon after his capture he experienced homosexual stirrings but resisted any overt expression for over a year. Eventually he formed an association with another prisoner and before his release he had a number of partners. He returned to his wife but continued with his overt homosexuality. Two years ago his wife divorced him and now, at the age of 38, he is living with another man and engaging in regular homosexuality.

There were other cases of individuals who had shown only weak tendencies in youth and as a result of their war experiences are now completely homosexual. There are also a few cases of individuals who can remember no homosexual impulses during adolescence, but who, nevertheless, have failed to revert to heterosexuality. These are probably examples of a latent tendency which may not have been aroused in more favourable circumstances. This situation is illustrated in the next history.

Case X. G—— was an R.A.F. officer aged 24 years by the time he was released, but he had a babyish face and could easily have been taken for 19 or 20. He was 21 at the time he was captured and without any homosexual experience.

"I cannot remember when I found out that some men were physically attracted to me but I know that long before the Jerries caught me, I had a lot of advances made to me and I had learnt how to take care of myself. At first I used to feel angry with these people who would try to get off with me, but after a time I grew more tolerant and just used to feel sorry for them. I was at six different Stalags in my first eight weeks of captivity and everywhere I went I received plenty of offers—from the German guards as well. But I just couldn't see it and even after I had been in the camp for over a year, I still didn't want anything to do with it. I masturbated a bit, but I always thought of girls at home when I did. . . .

"Most of the time I knocked around with Jack. He was about two years older than me, easy to get along with and we seemed to have a lot in common. We had been friends for quite a few weeks when one day I found myself watching Jack as he dozed on his bunk. I seemed to notice for the first time what strong muscular legs he had and what a fine smooth athletic body. I shocked myself with these thoughts because I swear it was the first time I had thought of Jack in that way. I kept trying to get those thoughts out of my mind. Just to prove to myself that I wasn't going queer, I spent half that night trying to get up a bit of excitement about a girl at home I used to be very fond of. It didn't work. From then on I could hardly bear to let Jack out of my sight and yet as soon as I saw him I cursed myself for thinking about him in that way. I even picked a quarrel with him so that he wouldn't tempt me by being near to me. But it was no good. I came to realize that I was in love with him, and that was that. I used to cry in bed at night, partly because I was angry with myself for letting this thing get the better of me after resisting so many temptations, and partly because it seemed such a hopeless kind of love anyway.

"I did my best to hide these thoughts from Jack. I was still ashamed of them and I thought it would break up our friendship. Then one day we were nailing something on to the wall when his cheek touched mine. A lot of the other boys used to creep up on me and do something like that, but not Jack. I didn't back away as I usually did, but stood still. I couldn't have moved if I had wanted to, I was trembling from head to foot. Slowly he turned his face round until our lips met.

"He told me he had longed to kiss me for weeks and weeks but he hadn't dared to try. I suppose I had got quite a reputation as an untouchable by that time. We kissed a lot of times after that and sometimes we did a bit more—nothing awful, you know what I mean. It wasn't just a way of relieving ourselves as it seemed to be with most of the others. I can't really explain it. All I can say is that I have never seen a girl and boy who love each other more than we do.

"What's going to happen now? I don't know. I don't think I can ever love a woman again. Perhaps I ought to try, but frankly I want to go back to Jack. And yet I want a family, children and all that sort of thing. And Jack is clever; I don't want to make a mess of his life. I don't know what I am going to do."

This history, like most of the others, was obtained at a Prisoner of War Rehabilitation Centre. The last that was heard of G——was that he had gone back to his friend and they were sharing a flat together.

Of course there were many who were successful in reverting to heterosexuality. It seems to depend partly upon the strength of the tendencies acquired in early childhood. It is well known that there is usually a certain amount of homosexual activity aboard a ship during long voyages into foreign waters, but the heterosexual activities of sailors when they return to port are even better known.

CHAPTER VII

SEXUAL BALANCE

In the first chapter of this section it was found that there was no convincing proof that there was any physical difference between most homosexuals and heterosexuals. Therefore it is difficult to see how inborn influences can be very important in the development of homosexual tendencies, except in the case of glandular disturbances. In rare cases these might be a major factor but more often they appear to be only a subordinate cause.

In Chapter IV the following early influences were found to be important:

> Dominance of mother, or absence of father.
> Absence of mother's love.
> Hostility of father.
> Faulty training during elimination learning.
> Strong feminine influences during childhood.
> Difficulty of fitting into masculine society.
> Segregation of sexes during adolescence.
> Ignorance in matters connected with sex.

These are the fundamental predisposing causes. They cover a wide area with the result that many, probably most, people have a homosexual component in their make-up. According to the impact of the early influences, so the tendency varies from very strong to very weak.

The next chapter on seduction brought out the following facts:

(1) That seduction will have little effect unless the seduced boy or man has previously developed homosexual tendencies.

(2) That a man with strong homosexual tendencies is sooner or later almost certain to meet up with a situation which will lead him into overt activities.

(3) So that the influence of seduction as a basic cause in homosexuality has been over-emphasized.

(4) But that, in so far as the homosexual tendency varies from individual to individual, an act of seduction may be the

turning-point in the homosexual career of males with only weak tendencies.

In Chapter VI we saw that when a man is thrown into an all-male environment for a long period, the incidence of homosexuality is very high. In such circumstances:

(1) Some men will have no overt experiences but a large percentage, including those with only a weak or latent homosexual tendency, will engage in some kind of homosexual behaviour.

(2) The extent of this behaviour will depend partly upon the length of the segregation, but more especially upon the strength of the tendencies acquired during childhood.

A study of these causes will reveal that far from being a unitary or isolated phenomenon, homosexuality is an extremely complicated psychological disease of widely varying manifestations. These homosexual leanings will occur in varying degrees in different individuals according to the early influences experienced by each child. And, because few people have had a completely smooth upbringing without the bumps of life that create emotional conflicts, most men will have a homosexual tendency to a greater or less extent. This is a fundamental point. All psychologists agree that there is no scientific basis for a precise classification of humans into heterosexuals and homosexuals; these are quantitative and qualitative variations.

Henry and Galbraith[35] report: "It should not be necessary to remark that the division of any group of human beings into those who are heterosexually adapted and those who are chiefly homosexual in their interests is somewhat arbitrary. Phylogenetically and embryologically it seems that we have evolved from a state of hermaphroditism and it would be unlikely, if not impossible, that any individual would lose all traces of bisexuality however mature he may become."

Dr. Karl Menninger[56] has said: "Psychoanalytically, we do not feel at all that homosexuality is the nasty little part of the individual which crops up now and then and with which some individuals are unfortunately afflicted to a more conspicuous extent. We take the position that everybody has in his personality a very large amount of homosexual demand, along with heterosexual demand."

So many things can contribute to the development of homosexual leanings that it becomes clear that homosexuality is not a clear-cut relatively rare condition. Its influence is present in nearly all men and expresses itself in their personality in some

57

way or other. The situation can best be envisaged as a sexual balance, and each individual falls somewhere in between the two extremes of heterosexuality and homosexuality.

Kinsey[45] made a thorough investigation into this balance and classified a very large number of people into seven grades. He added an eighth grade of people who appeared to have no socio-sexual contacts whatever. The other people were classified into their respective grades after a full investigation into their sex history, including both their overt experiences and their psycho-sexual reactions.

X class=no socio-sexual contacts.

o class=exclusively heterosexual.

1 class=predominantly heterosexual, only incidentally homosexual.

2 class=predominantly heterosexual, but more than incidentally homosexual.

3 class=equally heterosexual and homosexual.

4 class=predominantly homosexual, but more than incidentally heterosexual.

5 class=predominantly homosexual, but incidentally heterosexual.

6 class=exclusively homosexual.

The figures below are cumulative percentages, i.e., showing percentages of the population (U.S.A.) who have been classified "at least 1", "at least 2", "at least 3", etc., for at least three years (passing experiences have been eliminated from the data by showing only classifications that have involved a period of at least three years after the male has turned sixteen).

Age of subject	No. of cases	Grades							
		X	0	1-6	2-6	3-6	4-6	5-6	6
16-55	4,275	1·5	75·6	22·9	19·6	13·7	10·4	8·0	6·2

From this it can be seen that almost a quarter of the population have recognizable homosexual tendencies. One in ten are predominantly homosexual and over one in twenty are exclusively homosexual.

The situation is in some ways analogous to the incidence of tuberculosis. Doctors say that many people have the germ inside them. Whether it will develop into the disease or not depends upon chance in the form of the environment in which they find themselves. In a similar way there is a chance factor in the development of homosexuality.

Although the list of possible causes is a long one, it is a good sign that all but one of them stem from environmental sources. If it is true that a homosexual is more often bred than born, it makes it much more likely that something can be done to find a cure for his disability. We have little opportunity to change hereditary factors, but we have a reasonable chance to control our environment. As the tendencies are usually activated by emotional conflicts in childhood, it may even be possible to prevent, or at least diminish, the development of these tendencies in future generations.

Section III

TREATMENTS AND CURES

CHAPTER VIII

SELF-SUGGESTION

MANY PEOPLE THINK OF the homosexual problem only as a moral question. These people would say that to indulge in homosexual activities is to give way to temptation. If this is so, the question of cure does not arise. A moral person merely resolves not to get caught up in such activities.

But this attitude reveals that the real causes have not been understood. It has been noted that the first tendencies are formed in early childhood. In no sense can the young boy be held responsible for difficulties and accidents in his family circle. And because the tendencies formed at that time may be strong or weak, or absent altogether, it follows that the moral fibre needed to resist later temptations will vary from individual to individual. The men with only weak tendencies will have little difficulty in keeping strictly to heterosexual activities; the men with the strongest tendencies will almost certainly fall into homosexual activities at some period of their lives.

It has been argued that the homosexual is, in one way, more moral than the normal human being.[31] Paradoxical as this may seem, there is some logic in such an argument. This abnormality, like most other psychological abnormalities, is an attempt to resolve an earlier emotional conflict. It will be remembered that the child up to 5 years of age has strong sexual impulses directed to objects within the family circle. The heterosexual impulses of infants are incestuous and these normal incestuous impulses may be partly or totally inhibited by hostility in one of the parents, or by jealousy of the father (i.e. dominance of the mother), and, in addition, by an unconscious incest barrier of anxiety and guilt. If this inhibition is complete, any form of normal adult heterosexuality appears not only undesirable, but highly immoral. In the subconscious of the homosexual, his renunciation of adult heterosexuality is a moral act. Homosexuality may not be right but it is not incestuous and, to him, it is the lesser of two evils. Hence we have this peculiar paradox in the inner mind of the homosexual in which his primitive unconscious morality drives him into abnormality.

The argument that all homosexuals are immoral cannot be upheld, but as this abnormality is a disorder of the mind, then it is not unreasonable to expect the mind to be the best instrument for controlling it. In that case, is not the best cure for homosexuality to be found in the exercise of will power and resolution? This is a fair question, so it is important to see what results can be obtained this way.

It has been tried and is being tried every day by hundreds of people. For every man who goes to a doctor or psychiatrist in the belief that it is a mental disease, there are ten who go to clergymen or other confidants to try to find spiritual and moral strength to resist their homosexual difficulties. Many more keep their troubles to themselves and try to fight their bewildering tendencies on their own.

The results of such efforts can be seen in the magistrates courts up and down the country in almost every week of the year. These are the very people who find themselves in trouble with the law. The pious men, the strong-minded men, the men who have established themselves in the community—those who least merit it—are the ones most likely to meet this misfortune. For years they have successfully fought their strong natural (to them) inclinations, then one lapse brings all the wrath of society upon their heads and makes them outcasts.

The human mind has a number of unconscious mechanisms for dealing with unpleasant or anti-social impulses. The most familiar of these mechanisms is repression. This is an inhibitory process; it renders unconscious what would otherwise be conscious. But it cannot eliminate these awkward impulses altogether. The best it can do is to imprison in the depths of the mind these impulses which would otherwise express themselves openly. The operation of this mechanism rarely meets with complete success. Repression has grave limitations; for repressed impulses tend, on the whole, both to remain qualitatively unchanged and to undergo a quantitative increase in the face of the barriers opposing their discharge. Repression thus tends to perpetuate at unconscious levels of the mind the very impulses which it is designed to control; and, in times of stress, these impulses are liable to break through in their original form but with greater strength. Such is the case when homosexuality suddenly manifests itself later in life in individuals whose previous record appears to provide no precedent for this abnormality.

Repression is an unconscious mechanism, but the same difficulties may arise when a strong sexual impulse is consciously suppressed. A priest may tell a homosexual that "denial" is the only "cure". Such advice can bring about the most unfortunate

64

results. The strong-willed men who resist the urge to follow their homosexual tendencies are frustrating their sexual impulses. These powerful impulses can be bottled up for a time, but they are liable to burst out suddenly under pressure. This applies to all people, heterosexual as well as homosexuals, but the results are far more disastrous when this pent-up drive breaks out and reveals itself as an abnormality.

This does not mean that young men are advised to give way to every sexual impulse. There is nothing about the homosexual drive which deprives the sufferers of the ability to restrain their sexual actions to a very large extent. Homosexuals differ from heterosexuals only in the direction of their sexual drive, not in the strength of their impulses. But the heterosexuals can usually guide their sexual behaviour into socially accepted channels. For the homosexuals this is impossible. They are forced into homosexual behaviour by exactly the same forces which drive on normal men to heterosexual behaviour. Nor do they obtain extra sexual satisfaction from their abnormality as many people seem to think. They obtain merely the same amount of pleasure that normal men obtain so much more easily by their normal sexuality.

Nor will it help the homosexual man to engage in a series of promiscuous heterosexual experiences. Least of all will marriage provide a solution. Yet many people do believe that they will be able to control their homosexual tendencies once they are married. There is no physical abnormality about most of these men and the unfortunate girl who is chosen more as a remedy than as a mate will not suspect that anything is amiss. The man may be able to perform the sexual act to his wife's satisfaction, but this is no guarantee of cure. The results of such a marriage can have the most dire consequences which will bring tragedy and shame not only upon the man, but upon the blameless wife and children.

But what about sublimation? In recent years it has become a popular idea that sexual energy can be diverted into other channels and rendered harmless. Unfortunately sublimation is an unconscious mechanism and therefore not a voluntary process. It can be a useful aid but it is rarely a full controlling factor. This is what Freud[9] had to say about sublimation:

"We possess the aptitude of sublimating and transforming our sexual activities into other activities of a psychically related character, but non sexual. This process cannot, however, be carried out to an unlimited extent any more than can the conversion of heat into mechanical work in our machines. A certain amount of direct sexual satisfaction is for most organizations indispensable, and the renunciation of this individually varying amount is punished by manifestations which we are compelled to regard as morbid."

This points out the biggest difficulty. Sublimation has been found to be ineffective unless the non-sexual activity has some close connection with the drive. They must be "activities of a psychically related character". It follows that men with homosexual tendencies will be attracted to work which involves close contact with boys or young men. While it is true that some homosexuals deliberately take up work in youth movements and the teaching professions in order to make opportunities for abnormal practices, in the vast majority of cases this choice is made as an unconscious attempt at sublimation.

The tragedy of this situation is that whereas the sublimation may be successful in some cases, in others the unconscious attempt to divert the abnormal impulses into socially approved channels has the effect of putting them in the way of temptation. Sometimes a man does not realize the power of these tendencies until after he has committed, on impulse, his first homosexual act, perhaps comparatively late in life. Hence the large number of men who come before the courts for taking advantage of boys and young men are not always "fiends and rogues" (to quote a recent remark from the Bench), but are often moral men who have made a real (unconscious) effort to sublimate their abnormal sexual drives.

Successful sublimation is naturally an invaluable factor, for it converts anti-social behaviour into socially-approved channels. But when the adult is faced with conscious homosexual problems, it is clear that the unconscious sublimatory system has not worked; consequently it cannot be regarded as a reliable substitute and it will not relieve the sexual tension in the individual.

The difficulty of curing homosexuality is that it is different from other sexual abnormalities (sadism, etc.) which are extreme forms and found in heterosexuals also. But this is an alteration in the direction of the very impulse itself. The desire for emotional physical love is the same as in the normal man, only the object of the love is abnormal. The range of sexual activity is as variable as that found in heterosexuals, from the very promiscuous to the men who have definite homosexual tendencies but have had no overt experience. Spiritual and moral advice to stop these activities is about as effective as advising a normal man to refrain from taking an interest in the opposite sex.

Not all homosexuals try to cure themselves by self-suggestion. Some of them seek and obtain as much sexual satisfaction as possible. In this, they are no different from some heterosexuals. Before very long the promiscuous homosexuals have learnt to recognize other homosexuals and so are much less likely to get into trouble. The tragic fact is that the decent, intelligent men who make a real effort to rid themselves of their abnormality by suggestion, will-power, resolution or religious inspiration, more often find themselves in the hands of the law and ostracized by their fellow men.

CHAPTER IX

PSYCHOTHERAPY

P𝗌𝗒𝖼𝗁𝗂𝖺𝗍𝗋𝗒 𝗁𝖺𝗌 𝗆𝖺𝖽𝖾 great advances in recent years. Not only has the treatment of all kinds of psychological disorders become more successful, but the general public has changed its attitude to mental sickness. True there are still people who believe there is some kind of stigma attached to psychiatric treatment, but most people now realize that mental diseases are not the same thing as congenital insanity and psychological disorders can be treated and, in many cases, cured.

As the causes of homosexuality are rooted in emotional conflicts acquired in early childhood, there seems every chance that psychiatrists have much to contribute to this problem. Indeed there are many cases on record where successful cures have been made but it is usually a long and difficult business.

Not the least of these difficulties is the cost of the treatment. Homosexuality is a severe mental sickness and usually requires long analytical psychotherapy. It requires the time of a highly skilled professional man and, in all but the simplest cases, is beyond the pocket of the average man.

Even if the question of expense is overcome, there are other difficulties to worry the psychiatrist. In fact most psychologists will admit that of all the various cases they meet, homosexuality present the most problems. Much of modern psychiatric treatment is founded on the principle of bringing the unconscious conflict to light; once the emotional conflict is presented to the conscious mind, the patient can alleviate or even resolve it. But even when the early experiences are made accessible to the consciousness of the homosexual, it does not often help the patient to banish his abnormality.

As the tendency is a variable factor in each individual, and this tendency can be reinforced by experiences in later life, the chances of cure depend very much upon the extent of the patient's experiences before coming to see the psychiatrist.

Generally speaking, the younger the patient, the better the chance of a cure. The weaker or stronger tendency, acquired before the age of 5, is already there, but the later environment influences tend to be less fixed in a boy or young man. Where the sexual abnormality has been organized and practised over a prolonged period, the results are much more uncertain.

There is also a better chance of a cure where the homosexual tendency is weak. For example; there are some people who are only troubled by homosexual tendencies while under the influence of alcohol. Where the balance is on the heterosexual side with only incidental homosexual tendencies, the outcome is more hopeful.

Again, where the abnormality is being caused by some neurotic forms of anxiety, it is sometimes possible to effect a comparatively quick cure by the removal of the secondary neurotic feature. Excessive shyness in a boy, fears of impotency or other unreal sex fears may act as a barrier to heterosexual relations. If the psychiatrist can remove that barrier, the patient will be able to rid himself of his homosexuality.

Where the practices are against the ethics or religious beliefs of the patient and he is eager to be cured, it is easier for the psychiatrist to proceed with the analysis.

Most mental diseases produce a state of great mental anxiety in the sufferer. Homosexuality is no exception, but as the years go by, the homosexual must adjust himself to his own disability if only for his own peace of mind. He will try to meet and mix with other homosexuals, if he can. Some homosexuals live in an almost exclusive homosexual society, speaking their own jargon, and formulating their own standards and values. Cure for these people would mean starting again in a new world with new friends.

Even the homosexuals who are living a normal life except for the occasional secret overt experiences are not eager to be cured if it means renouncing all sexual activities. A homosexual gets no more, but no less satisfaction out of his sexual experiences than the average man. A confirmed homosexual would regard this kind of cure in much the same way as a heterosexual would regard the suggestion that he give up all his sexual activities.

The desire to be cured is not something that can be expected from the older homosexual who has managed to adjust himself to his abnormality. Nevertheless the majority of homosexuals would welcome the opportunity to rid themselves of these socially condemned impulses. Even then there is no guarantee of cure. It is not correct that all homosexuals could be cured if only they wanted to be.

Although there are a large number of successful cures being made each year, there remains a large group for whom there is little hope. The man who has never had any heterosexual experience may respond well to treatment, for here the psychiatrist is trying to develop an unknown potentiality. But the older man who has mixed with women for a number of years but never felt any sexual desire for any of them is unlikely to be a successful case.

The man with feminine characteristics also presents a difficult case. Such characteristics may not be inborn, but they are a sure indication that there is a strong feminine influence in his environment. It is unlikely that anything less than a complete change of his work, his home and his whole social life will be effective.

The physical and mechanical techniques, such as insulin shock treatment, electric convulsive treatment and prefrontal leucotomy, are not more successful in finding a cure than the analytical methods. Owensby[60] has reported six cases of curing homosexuality by shock treatment using metrazol, but the case reported by Liebman[50] is more typical. One of his patients suffered from transvestism, psychosis and homosexuality. Electro-shock treatment cured the first two but had no effect on the patient's homosexual tendencies except that he is now·more mindful of social conventions and makes some attempt to conceal his abnormality. On the whole, it seems unlikely that this mental disorder which is rooted in the early emotional conflicts of childhood can be cured by shock treatment or brain surgery.

It can be seen, therefore, that the results of psychiatric treatment are successful only when a careful selection of cases is made beforehand. The old, the adjusted, the feminine and those with strong tendencies are, for the most part, beyond the reach of complete cure at the present state of psychological knowledge.

With the possible exception of the desire to be cured, the various factors which make the results uncertain are all beyond the conscious control of the homosexual. But the position of these men is not hopeless. This section has been dealing only with the possibilities of a complete cure. In the next section, it will be seen that psychotherapy can at least lighten the load and teach these men to understand and control their abnormality.

Meanwhile it is important to note that although the number of homosexuals who can be completely cured is strictly limited, there are many who could and should be treated, but for one reason or another have been unable to get psychiatric assistance.

CHAPTER X

UNDERSTANDING AND CONTROL

ALTHOUGH THE PSYCHIATRIST cannot guarantee a cure in a number of cases, almost every homosexual would benefit from some form of psychotherapy. A number of the most skilled psychiatrists believe that it is risky to try to re-direct the behaviour of the older, more established homosexual into patterns which are foreign to the background of the patient. It may even lead to the development of other psychological disorders; in these cases the psychiatrist can only help the individual to accept himself and control his disability.

In this respect, the psychiatrist is not bound by the pretended social code of the community. If the patient can be fitted into the pattern of the particular group to which he belongs, it will, at least, enable him to control his abnormality without doing harm to others. A cure may not be possible but it is often possible to help the patient to live a useful life without coming into open conflict with society.

Our society has selected as the decreed path for all humanity one that is too narrow to be congenial to all temperaments. Sometimes the standard temperament chosen by society is not even the temperament enjoyed by the majority. For example, our sex code decrees that a well-behaved person is virtually sexless before marriage. This may be ethically and morally desirable, but most people are aware that it does not work in practice. Human nature is remarkably adaptable, and so most people can keep up the outward signs that society demands. But there is still left a large minority that cannot be moulded into this standard shape.

It is useless to try to re-shape the temperaments of these people. All the pressures of society have failed to do this. It is far better to try and understand and control these deviations from the standard and encourage them to make their contribution to the community welfare. Sometimes the deviation itself gives the individual a special insight into the solution of a particular problem, or helps him to develop special gifts which contribute to the general happiness. Many sociologists believe that a small

71

percentage of homosexual personalities are desirable in any culture; the homosexual produces imaginative and creative originalities that seem beyond the ability of the heterosexual.

But the socially conscious homosexual, anxious to play his part in the world, is the one most likely to experience frustration. As a result of society's attitude to his disability, he will tend to repress his sexual impulses with the unfortunate results noted in Chapter VIII.

But there are factors other than repression and sublimation which help to control difficult and anti-social impulses. Of these the most important is the influence of the ego. At birth the child is a creature of unorganized impulses, ignorant of the essential demands of life except at a very primitive instinctual level. As he becomes older, he learns by experience and gradually he finds out what is allowed and what is prohibited. His instinctive impulses become modified in such a way as to make his behaviour better adapted to the conditions of life; a certain order is introduced into his emotional life with a view to avoiding conflicts of feeling. These changes are all the work of the developing ego.

Now the ego develops both consciously and unconsciously; it is largely influenced by the example set by the parents and the knowledge that the child gains about himself. The success with which the individual's impulses are regulated in deference to social demands will depend upon the extent to which the ego is developed upon sound and sensible lines. The correctly developed ego will help the individual to acquire insight into his own motives, to tolerate the frustration of his desires, to modify his impulses in the light of outer circumstances and generally adapt his behaviour to the conditions of life.

But this development of the ego depends upon a true understanding and a conscious recognition of these wayward impulses. This is where the psychiatrist can help the man with homosexual tendencies. Psychotherapy can help the individual to understand his abnormality and to control it so that it will not hinder his attempts to fit into the accepted social pattern.

There is one other kind of treatment which is also more of a control than a cure. This is still in the early stages of research and it would be unwise to make far-reaching claims at this time. However the possibilities are interesting and it is worthwhile reporting the results obtained so far.

The most important research into the effects of female hormone injection upon sexual offenders has been done by Sessions Hodge.[65] He administered very large doses of oestrone (female sex hormone) to persons convicted of sexual offences who were given treatment on their own request. Later he treated other

72

people who had not been convicted but were suffering from some sexual abnormality. Fifteen cases have been treated so far, all of whom had requested it in writing after the nature of the treatment and its probable consequences had been explained. Here are two cases quoted in the *Medico-Legal Journal*:

"Male aged 51 years, had two convictions for indecent assault on male persons. An intelligent man in good position, it was considered that he was a schizoid personality and his deviation was of long standing and he himself not amendable to psychotherapy. Oestrone treatment abolished sexual libido, and he was discharged to ordinary life within two months of the institution of treatment. Eighteen months later he is reported to be in full gainful occupation and no longer 'concerned with sexual feelings'."

"Male aged 37 years who came voluntarily, being concerned by his definite homosexual bias which, though it had not since puberty found overt expression, was nevertheless a source of great worry and unhappiness. The man was of superior intelligence and culturally and ethically of good status. He appeared after close investigation to be a homosexual deviant of very long standing . . . and he failed to respond to psychotherapy. Treatment by oestrone has been followed by loss of sexual libido and he reports considerable 'mental relief'."

All the cases treated showed a suppression of sexual feeling. The response to dosage varied with each individual, but a reaction can be expected within six weeks of the start of the treatment. The effect could be varied from diminishing to totally abolishing all sexual desire and activity. In observations lasting as long as eight years it had been found that sexual desire was absent so long as maintenance doses were continued. It was found to return in about two weeks if the patient stopped taking the oestrone. Injections of male sex hormones three times weekly were found to restore the sexual potency while the oestrone treatment was continuing. By this means the effect of the treatment can be graded and even reversed.

In the group treated by Hodge, the suppression of sexual desire was complete. The patients reported that they felt no arousal even in situations which were known to be stimulating previously. They were a varied group consisting of different occupations, cultural backgrounds and levels of intelligence. Some had been convicted of heterosexual or homosexual offences, others had sexual abnormalities but have never been convicted. All have agreed that they experienced a relief and release from an all-pervading difficulty. All have been able to work better since their treatment as they no longer are preoccupied with impulses which have proved either actually or potentially dangerous. As the doses required varied from patient to patient, the expense of the treatment also varied but the average cost was about 16s. a week.

It is interesting to note that the injection of female hormones had just the same effect on very feminine passive homosexuals as on virile homosexuals. It diminished the sexual desire in all cases. This treatment had no effect upon women sexual offenders and the injection of male hormones in women increased their sexual activities, as it does with men. The injection of male hormones in effeminate men will not turn them into virile men but merely increase their sexual activity.

The results to date are encouraging but there are certain disadvantages. This cannot be classed as a cure, for the patient has to continue to take the oestrone indefinitely. Soon after he gives up the maintenance doses, his sexual desires will return. He could nullify the treatment by taking male sex hormones, if he knew where to get them.

The present restoration of function occurs within two or three weeks, but it seems possible that prolonged doses of oestrone will eventually degenerate the testicles and lead to permanent infertility. This may be the desired result in the case of the long-standing infanto-homosexuals, but it is a powerful weapon to put into the hands of the Court if it is ever used without the patient's consent. It is a form of glandular castration and its possible use in the hands of a dictator with racial prejudices can be imagined.

There is no certain cure for homosexuality. In the first section it was emphasized that will-power and self-suggestion without professional advice are of little value. In many cases, their use involves the bottling up of powerful drives which can lead to the break-out of a sudden impulse. As it is the conscientious, intelligent and religious men who usually try to control their drives by these methods, the result is that some of our best citizens are disgraced and ostracized by the community.

Psychological treatment is successful in a number of cases. When the patient is young, when he wishes to be cured, where the inherent tendency is weak and where the environment has not become an important factor, the chances of a successful cure are good. It appears to be as difficult to change a complete homosexual into a complete heterosexual as it would be to accomplish the opposite feat.

74

In cases where the sexual impulses cannot be diverted into heterosexual channels, psychotherapy can be used to alleviate the difficulties and bring them under control. These homosexual impulses, often as distressing to the patient himself as to society in general, can then be understood and the patient can be relieved of any added neurosis caused by these difficulties.

For those men whose condition is such that psychotherapy is not enough to enable them to gain control over their abnormality, a new technique of oestrone injections is being developed which will nullify all sexual desire and activities.

THE EFFECTIVENESS OF THE LAW

CHAPTER XI

IN THE PAST

H OMOSEXUALITY HAS BEEN found in all civilizations and among all people of whom there is a record, but the laws of the different communities have varied considerably. At times it has been approved and encouraged, at others it has been condemned and punished very severely.

Much of the culture and political ideas of Western civilization has been inherited from the Greeks whose liberal ideas on sex are well known. But the sex code of Western civilization is inherited almost entirely from the Jews through the Christian Churches.

The Jews were a struggling race who urgently needed to expand. The outstanding feature of ancient Jewish sex life was the desire for offspring. They encouraged polygamy and were proud of the fact that Solomon had a thousand wives. The many "begats" in the Old Testament are an example of the high esteem in which reproduction was held. By Jewish law a man was required to marry his brother's childless widow and raise up children for him. Any sexual activity that did not produce children was condemned—this included withdrawal, the ancient equivalent of birth-control. Homosexuality was regarded with intense abhorrence and was punished by death. Almost any kind of sex behaviour was better than this abnormality. For example, there is the story of Lot (Gen. xix) who, when the men of Sodom were besieging the house and demanding to be given two angels for homosexual practices, offered the mob his daughters instead. In the Book of Judges, there is an account of a concubine being given to the mob of men instead of a man they were demanding for homosexual purposes (Judges xix).

The Christians took over this attitude from the Jews and under Christianized Roman Law, homosexuals were either burnt to death or reeds were driven into their bladders until they died of this torture.

The Ecclesiastical Courts of early English history decreed that sodomy was a crime for which the penalty was death. It did not become a felony and thus subject to ordinary criminal jurisdiction until the reign of Henry VIII. A few years after the dissolution of the monasteries, the Statute of 1533 made the offence a felony, punishable by death. This Statute was repealed in 1547 by Edward VI, re-enacted in 1548, repealed in 1553 and re-enacted in 1562. The offence remained a capital punishment for the next 275 years until Sir Robert Peel, then Home Secretary, abolished the death penalty for this and many other offences in 1828. The death penalty remained in Scotland until 1889.

An Italian visitor named von Archenholtz[6] writes in 1787 "Since English women are so beautiful and the enjoyment of them is so general, the revulsion of these Islanders against sodomy passes all bounds. Attempted homosexuality is punished by the pillory and several years' imprisonment, the act itself by the gallows. The pillory, however, is almost as good as death."

That Archenholtz did not exaggerate about the pillory is shown in these extracts from a newspaper report of 1810.[25] In that year a meeting-place was discovered in Vere Street. Seven men were found guilty and sentenced to imprisonment and the pillory in Haymarket opposite Panton Street. These extracts describe what happened after the trial:

"Shortly before 12 noon the 'ammunition carts' started from the neighbouring market places. These were a number of carts drawn by butcher boys, who had previously filled them with offal and dung from the slaughter houses. Street vendors were also in readiness, carrying on their heads baskets filled with rotten apples, pears, cabbages and other vegetables and corpses of dogs and cats. All these articles were sold at high prices to the onlookers, who spared no expense in order to provide themselves with missiles. A group of fishwives were there, armed with stinking flaunders and decaying guts. But these were not sold, as their zealous owners wished to keep them for their own use. . . .

"Long before any of them [the prisoners] reached the places where the pillories awaited them, their faces were totally disfigured by blows, missiles and mud, and looked like living dung hills. About fifty women obtained permission to form a circle round them, and these incessantly bombarded them with rotten potatoes and eggs, with dead cats, offal, mud and dung from slop-pails and buckets brought by some butchers of St. James Market. . . .

"They were fettered and sealed in such a manner that they could not lie down and at the most could only protect their heads to a limited extent from the missiles by bending them. Some of them were badly injured by brick bats and their faces bled horribly. The streets through which they passed reverberated with the shouts and curses hurled at them by the mob."

80

Although the actions of this mob cannot be defended, it was the State and the legal authorities who provoked the outrage. Such measures are barbarous and unworthy of a civilized country, even 150 years ago. It is difficult to imagine any more horrible tortures or severer penalties, but it is noteworthy that these measures were not at all successful in stamping out the practice of homosexuality.

The Offences Against the Person Act was passed in 1861 and this imposed the maximum sentence of penal servitude for life. This Act is still on the Statute Book.

If it can be assumed that penal servitude is less severe than the death penalty, it can be said that some progress toward a humane attitude was being made. But in 1886 a new development occurred. Up to that time, the laws had only punished sodomy, paederasty (sodomy committed against a boy) and attempted sodomy or paederasty. Now under Section 11 of the Criminal Law Amendment Act of 1885, homosexual relations of any kind were made criminal even if the offences were practised in private.

The Bill was part of a campaign against prostitution and white slavery and in its original draft had no mention of homosexuality. Section 11 was incorporated after the briefest discussion in the House and it is doubtful if the Members of Parliament understood the full implications of the law they were making. Sir Travers Humphreys tells the story of the birth of Section 11 in his Preface to *The Trials of Oscar Wilde*:[40]

"Until that Act came into force, on January 1st, 1886, the criminal law was not concerned with alleged indecencies between grown-up men committed in private. Everyone knew that such things took place, but the law only punished acts against public decency and conduct tending to the corruption of youth. The Bill in question entitled 'A Bill to make further provision for the protection of women and girls, the suppression of brothels and other purposes', was introduced and passed by the House of Lords without any reference to indecency between males. In the Commons, after a second reading without comment, it was referred to a committee of the whole House. In committee Mr. Labouchere moved to insert in the Bill the clause which ultimately became Section 11 of the Act, creating the new offence on indecency between male persons in public *or private*. Such conduct in public was, and always has been, punishable at common law. There was no discussion except that one member asked the Speaker whether it was in order to introduce at that stage a clause dealing with a totally different class of offence to that against which the Bill was directed. The Speaker having ruled that anything could be introduced by leave of the House, the clause

81

was agreed to without further discussion, the only amendment moved being one by Sir Henry James with the object of increasing the maximum punishment from 12 to 24 months, which was also agreed to without discussion.

"It is doubtful whether the House fully appreciated that the words 'in public or private' in the new clause had completely altered the law; but as soon as the Royal Assent had been given and the Act was published, there began a spate of correspondence in the newspapers, both legal and lay, and references to the subject on various public platforms, which were duly reported. A learned Recorder dubbed it 'The Blackmailer's Charter', and an eminent Q.C. prophesied that juries would refuse to convict where the alleged acts were in private and not visible to any member of the public. On the other hand those interested in the welfare of girls welcomed the Act as a whole so warmly (and indeed it was an excellent Act apart from Section 11), and it was so clearly impossible to do anything except let the law take its course, that after a few weeks the clamour died down and the public interest became centred upon some more savoury topic."

So the Bill that has provided thousands of pounds for hundreds of blackmailers in the last fifty years and inflicted the acutest agony of mind on millions of people was passed without forethought and without discussion, and it is still the law of the land to-day.

CHAPTER XII

THE LAW TO-DAY

Persons found guilty of homosexual offences to-day are punished either under Section 61 or 62 of the Offences Against the Person Act of 1861, or under Section 11 of the Criminal Law Amendment Act of 1885. The 1861 Act states:

"Whoever shall be convicted of the abominable crime of buggery, committed either with mankind or any animal, shall be liable, at the discretion of the Court to be kept in penal servitude for life or for any term not less than ten years."

Section 62 of the same Act states:

"Whoever shall attempt to commit the said abominable crime, or shall be guilty of any assault with intent to commit the same, or any indecency on any male person, shall be guilty of an misdemeanour and being convicted thereof shall be liable, at the discretion of the Court, to be kept in penal servitude for any term not exceeding ten years and not less than three years, or to be imprisoned for any term not exceeding two years, with or without hard labour."

It is difficult to obtain proof of sodomy having taken place, but Section 62 provides against an attempt, an assault or any indecency. Under the recent Criminal Justice Act, penal servitude and hard labour have been abolished but the maximum penalty is still imprisonment for life. Except in the case of assault, the passive party if over 16 is also guilty.

Gross indecency between male persons is a misdemeanour under Section 11 of the Criminal Law Amendment Act of 1885 and is punishable with two years' imprisonment. This Act is used where there is no evidence of sodomy and covers all forms of mutual masturbation and oral practices. The fact that the activities are performed in private with the knowledge and consent of both parties does not legitimize the offence. If one of the partners is under 16, the fact that he has passed puberty (this is a legitimate offence with a girl) does not lessen the offence. If both partners are over 16, they are considered to be equally guilty.

In many cases the rooms of the accused are searched and

letters, photographs or other evidence are produced to show that the accused has homosexual tendencies. The admission of such evidence is often allowed in spite of the rule—"that evidence is not admissible merely to prove that the persons accused has a genial propensity to commit a crime similar in character to that with which he is charged".

It is also a misdemeanour for a man to appear in public in women's clothes (but not vice versa). Cases where men have handled other men or interfered with their clothing are treated as "assaults" and come under Section 62 of the 1861 Act.

That is the law as it stands to-day. Both laws were formulated long before the discoveries of modern psychology. Little was known about mental disease in those days and medical men had not then come to regard homosexuality as a sickness of the mind.

Medicine is a dynamic science. The doctor must be prepared to throw over long-held convictions and adopt new ideas and new methods. The law is static and conservative. It has been built up bit by bit through the centuries, often to meet situations that no longer exist or have now widely changed. Furthermore, the law is administered in the main by elderly people who find it more difficult to adapt their thinking to recent social changes and modern scientific discoveries.

Magistrates and judges tend to regard the homosexual as a particularly revolting kind of criminal. As many of these cases are not reported, the public is not always aware that homosexual offences are still being punished very severely in some places, particularly in rural areas.

The case that follows is quoted from a paper by Taylor, the medical officer of Brixton Prison:[72]

Case XI. Aged 48 years. Importuning; no previous convictions. This man was a fine-looking specimen, alert and intelligent, and a bank cashier by profession. He was single and supported an aged mother. He had realized he was a homosexual for as long as he could remember. He was not attracted to women, but was friendly with many and did occasionally dance with them. He had a sincere affection for his mother. Homosexual activity had only once gone further than mutual masturbation. He had on this occasion played the passive partner in peno-rectal intercourse, but was so revolted that it was never repeated. He had a strong guilt complex following mutual masturbation; the fantasy during nocturnal emissions was one of self-masturbation. He was charged with importuning and admitted the offence. He had, however, indulged over-freely in alcohol, and this was the first occasion on which he had ever committed such an act. He was allowed bail

84

and attempted suicide before his appearance in court, but was saved by his mother. He had originally intended to murder her first but found himself unable to do so, though he killed the cat as a start to wiping out the entire family. Considerable time was spent with this man before he went to court, and an attempt was made to re-educate him, with some success. It was strongly recommended to the court that therapy might help to alleviate his anxiety and sense of guilt and reorientate him to society.

Prison life on this "mother's boy" will inflict a trauma that he will carry with him to the grave. But his greatest punishment awaits him after he has left the prison and attempts to take up the threads of his life again. The next case is less typical, but by no means unusual.

Case XII. This man was 43 years, single and of previous good character. He was charged with misbehaviour with a 23-year-old Guardsman at his own flat. He asked for seven other offences with soldiers to be taken into consideration. The police had kept a watch on the man's flat and saw through a window what had taken place. The man had given the soldiers cigarettes, drinks and sums of money. The magistrate said that the case revealed the corruption of young soldiers who were otherwise decent young men. He told the accused that he was lacking in self-control and self-discipline, that psychiatric treatment would be provided "if necessary" but that it was really up to the man to rescue himself. The soldier was told to cleanse himself by hard work. The older man was sentenced to eighteen months' imprisonment and the soldier was bound over.

If it is possible to believe that this man really corrupted eight innocent guardsmen, then eighteen months' imprisonment is probably not a long enough sentence. It is much more likely that all of the soldiers knew exactly why they were invited to the man's flat; such men usually demand payment before they take part in any homosexual activities. It raises the question as to which party is really the most guilty—the man who is obviously a complete homosexual with the means to be able to pay for some meagre sexual satisfaction in his own private room, or the soldiers who may have no strong homosexual tendencies but are prepared to prostitute themselves at the expense of a man who is suffering from a mental disorder.

CHAPTER XIII

IMPRISONMENT

As imprisonment is the fate of most convicted homosexuals, it is worth while seeing what can happen to them when they are sent to prison. It has already been noted that one of the causes of homosexuality was a restricted all-male environment and some of the experiences of the prisoners in the last war were quoted. One must not expect as high a moral outlook in a prison where only convicted criminals are quartered and the resistance to homosexual temptations can be expected to be correspondingly less.

Dr. Barnes, a prison doctor, has said: "If one were consciously to plan an institution perfectly designed to promote sexual degeneracy, he would create the modern prison." Two psychologists, Henry and Gross,[36] have stated that the prison is the ideal place to produce homosexuality. They add: "The advent of a homosexual in many prisons is welcomed as a godsend by many of the inmates". Fishman[24], the Chief Inspector of Federal Prisons in the United States, has estimated that 30-40 per cent. of the inmates of the prisons are homosexual and will indulge at the first convenient opportunity.

Every year a large number of boys, adolescent youths and young men, sent to prison for other than sex crimes, become homosexual either temporarily or permanently. Much of this is caused by the lack of normal sexual outlets and by the fact that the proportion of other homosexuals is probably higher within a prison than in the outside world. There is one much more serious cause which prison authorities are reluctant to admit. A new prisoner without strong homosexual tendencies, who might otherwise have avoided these activities, may be forced into homosexual practices through fear.

Prisoners have their strict codes of behaviour as every warden knows. These are particularly powerful where the prison contains a high percentage of perennial criminals. The worst possible transgression against this code is to be branded as "a stool"—report on the activities of the other prisoners. Prisoners who are suspected of telling tales about the other inmates can have their life made unbearable no matter how watchful the authorities may be. In such a situation, it is quite possible for an older prisoner to seduce a new prisoner and frighten him into keeping quiet about it.

One prisoner told Fishman[24] of the time when he was sharing a cell with an old time prisoner named W——. This is how he described the first night and subsequent events:

"W—— had a long stiletto hidden inside the drain-pipe held to the little cross bar with a piece of string. He suddenly turned and held this stiletto about three inches away from me and said that if I ever told anybody anything that went on in the cell he would run the knife through my heart. . . . That night I was tight asleep and I was suddenly awakened with the feeling of a weight on me. . . . W—— had turned me before I wakened so that I was lying on my stomach and he kept the point of the stiletto blade against my shoulder with one hand and whispered that he would run it through me if I let out a sound. I guess I was a coward but I let him do what he wanted. . . . During the rest of the time I was there this happened once or twice a week. Sometimes he made me practise mutual masturbation with him. Usually it was sodomy."

Although the prison authorities do their best to stamp out any signs of homosexuality and any prisoner caught is severely punished, they are unable to make much progress when the victims are frightened to expose the seducers. The same difficulties are experienced in the Borstal institutions and it is alleged that old prisoners are able to spot ex-Borstal boys soon after they arrive in prison.

Even without fear or threats, the restriction of any kind of normal sexual outlet puts a heavy strain upon the prisoner, no matter how slight his tendencies may be. In his book, *Prison Days and Nights*, Victor Nelson[57] tells the story of Barton. The author first met this boy when they were both fourteen. He describes him as a "rough, tough boy who was always getting into trouble. At this time, Barton was a perfectly normal boy sexually. Of this I am certain." They met again ten years later and to Nelson's surprise, "no longer was he the eternal trouble-maker. He had become well-behaved, gentle, almost effeminate. . . . Barton was pathetically eager to make me understand that his decline into homosexuality was totally unpremeditated. . . . The shock of discovery that he had become homo completely changed his whole character. He gradually developed an intense feeling of inferiority. And although he managed to conceal it from his friends, it hurt him in a hundred irreparable ways. He lost his utter self-confidence, which had always been one of his most pronounced traits. . . . Barton celled with six or eight other inmates for longer or shorter periods. He told me that most of them, even those who professed to entertain the most violent prejudices towards homosexuality, eventually participated with him in some form of abnormal sexual activity. Thus Barton, having himself gone homo, was instrumental in leading other men down the same dark road. Barton was still in prison when I was released, and had become so thoroughly steeped in homosexuality that I doubt if he will ever go back to normal intercourse. A bit of wreckage from the sea of crime, he will be washed up on the shores of some community whose waters he will help to pollute."

The fate of the man sent to prison for a homosexual offence can be expected to be more complicated in this respect than of those in prison for other offences. But his prison experience is just the beginning of his troubles. Society still has to take its revenge when he has left the prison gates behind. The difficulties of getting back and starting a new life are so great that it is no wonder that many men give up the attempt to live by the socially approved codes and abandon themselves to open homosexuality.

CHAPTER XIV

THE RESULTS

Some progress has been made in modifying the legal attitude to homosexuality. Under the Criminal Justice Act of 1948, the conditions of probation have been extended and improved. The court may now order treatment under a qualified medical practitioner and some magistrates, particularly in urban areas, are remanding homo- sexual first offenders for psychological treatment. Already there are on record a number of cases that have resulted in complete cures, and which, if dealt with by some other law officers, might have been punished by years of imprisonment. Some men have become potentially good citizens where, in less fortunate cases, they would have become jail-birds and a burden to the whole community.

The severity of the punishments varies from a remand for treatment to fifteen years' imprisonment. Much depends upon the understanding of the magistrate or judge; if the law officer's own sex education has been free from puritanical influences and if he has attempted to keep up to date with the modern discoveries of psychology, then he is likely to take a more enlightened attitude when dealing with offences that stem from a disease of the mind.

Sometimes the judge will assure the offender and everyone else that adequate treatment will be given in prison. In 1943, only eighteen out of 3,392 persons found guilty of sexual offences were given a full course of treatment. Only six out of twenty-eight medical officers had even had the diploma in psychiatry.[2] Since then there has been slight improvement, but there is still a great shortage of full-time medically qualified psychiatrists to give the necessary treatment in the prisons.

Also the conditions inside a prison make it much more difficult for the psychiatrist to do his work. In the *British Medical Journal*,[66] Stanley-Jones writes: "To commit a cultured invert to the soul-crushing experience of a long term of penal servitude, where his only contact with the opposite sex is an occasional sight of the prison charwoman, is as futile from the point of view of treatment as to hope to rehabilitate a chronic alcoholic by giving him occupational therapy in a brewery."

Another difficulty that psychiatrists have to face is that even some of the finest legal minds consider treatment to have failed if it does not produce a complete cure. It is not safe to predict that every case will respond to treatment, but it is safe to say that they will invariably fail to respond to imprisonment. Many cases have shown improvement after psychological treatment although the offender's abnormality may not have been entirely re-directed.

Quite often it is impossible to remove the patient's desire or appetite in the time available but help can be given in its understanding and control. The psychologist will try to work out with the patient the reasons he has developed homosexual tendencies, and the reasons that heterosexual development did not occur. By these means the patient may be able to see how old situations in which, perhaps, his parents were involved are still affecting him. He can be shown how certain environmental influences are still operative in keeping his abnormality active and he can be shown how to change or combat these influences.

It is unreasonable to expect that even in favourable cases, the improvement will necessarily be immediate. Homosexuality is a disease rooted in the earliest years of the man; sometimes it is a matter of weeks before the psychiatrist can find and analyse these basic causes. This may produce a difficult situation when the offender, remanded for treatment, repeats the offence during the early stages of the treatment. It is quite wrong to assume that because the offence is repeated during treatment the case should be written off as a failure. It is no more reasonable to assume that homosexuality can be cured by a magical wave of the psychological wand than to expect immediate recovery from tuberculosis upon entering a clinic.

The psychological treatment of homosexual offenders has not yet become widespread enough to make it possible to collect statistically reliable data. In one clinic, forty-five men have been given treatment, of whom three have been re-convicted. Present reports indicate that a number of complete cures have been achieved in cases remanded for treatment, but cures of cases treated in prison are disappointingly low. But most cases selected for treatment have shown some improvement, though this, too, is subject to wide variation. The psychological treatment of homosexual offenders has not turned out to be the miracle cure that some misguided enthusiasts had prophesied. It can be said, however, that it is the only constructive method known to us at the present time.

The final purpose of the law is to protect the people of the nation. Crimes are committed when other people are harmed. It is worth while asking what is being achieved by inflicting harsh punishments on homosexual offenders. The two main objects of the law seem to be: (1) to stamp out all homosexual activities, (2) to protect other people from these activities.

It has been noted that throughout history the harsh treatment has had very little effect. It is even possible that the heavy penalties have added an extra spice to the pursuit of these practices. The Duchess of Orleans[70] commented on the prevalence of homosexuality in England during the reign of William III. She wrote: "You ask why people persist in tasting such forbidden pleasure, but since the days of Adam it has always been so, that forbidden fruits taste better than those that are allowed." Oscar Wilde[76] referred to his activities: "It is like feasting with panthers. The danger is half the excitement." Kenneth Walker[74] in his book, *Physiology of Sex*, writes: "In France during the old Monarchy when a homosexual, as the law then stood, was liable to be burnt at the stakes, inversion was both fashionable and conspicuous, whereas in modern France, under the Napoleonic code, homosexuality is looked down upon and very little in evidence. The mere fact that there are harsh laws against an activity may lead to a glorification of it."

It would be wrong to assume that the danger of conviction acts as an added incentive to most homosexuals, but it may well be that the law indirectly encourages these activities, simply by making too much of them. Certainly the existing laws do not seem to be a very effective deterrent. Our prisons would not be large enough to hold all those who actually violate this law but do not get caught. If every male who has ever committed a homosexual offence were to be imprisoned, there would be almost as many men in prison as out.

The severity of the penalties seems to have little to do with the incidence. In the United States, the law varies in each state. The penalty is twenty years in New York, one to ten years in California, one to three years in Virginia. A fine of 2,000 dollars and/or five years is the penalty in Louisiana; in Georgia, the penalty is imprisonment for life, and it is not considered a crime in Vermont and the District of Columbia. The laws of the other states are equally varied. Yet no correlation can be found between the severity and the incidence of homosexuality—and this is in a country where there are no barriers between the states.

The second object of the law is to protect other people. The man who seduces young boys or the man who uses force or trickery to obtain his ends, is a menace to the community and society has a right to demand protection. He is no better, and no worse, than the man who seduces young girls or the man who rapes a woman. In these cases, the offender may still have a mental disease, but the community must be protected from such outrages even at the price of taking away the liberty of the man with the diseased mind.

But sending a man to prison is not enough. A sentence of five years' imprisonment on a man who has committed paederasty is like saying to him: We shall see that you do not do this for another five years. It does not do anything to prevent the same thing happening all over again in five years' time. A man gives up many of his civil rights when he goes to prison, but one right he does not lose is the right to be treated for a severe disease, physical or psychological. One man who had twice been convicted for homosexual offences served two terms of imprisonment without any suggestion concerning treatment being made to him. When he was arrested for the third time, he maintained that as he had twice been in prison without anything being done to cure him, he should be treated as a first offender. His argument is not illogical.

Little is gained if the law is content to restrict the activities of such people. When the sentences have been served what guarantee has society that the offence will not be repeated? Imprisonment aggravates rather than cures the abnormality. These offenders may have learnt enough to avoid capture in the future, but they will not cease their activities as a result of their imprisonment. Some of them will now bear a grudge against society and turn to blackmailing.

It follows that psychological treatment should be given to homosexual offenders wherever there seems a slight chance of its helping the individual—and that means nearly every case. The chances of curing him may not be good, but at least it may be possible for him to control his abnormality so that he is no longer a liability to the community. It will be argued that this is making life too easy for the offender. In the same way, it was argued that penicillin should not be used for the treatment of syphilis because it cured the disease too easily. The argument for psychological treatment of homosexuals can be summarized in this simple question and answer: Do we want to prevent a recurrence of the offence? If so, we know of only one way we can do this, and that is by psychological treatment—and even this method cannot be guaranteed to work.

Democracy can be very intolerant of small minorities and when this law was made, it was thought that homosexuality was an uncommon and unusual perversion. It has now become clear that, in this country alone, thousands are continuously wrestling with this difficulty and millions have had more than a casual experience of these activities. The very frequency of it must sooner or later cause some alteration in the law. Any law which is so remote from the real habits of the people that it turns over a quarter of the male population into secret criminals cannot be said to be fitted to the needs and lives of the men it governs.

In a later section (Chapter XXVI), it will be suggested that some distinction could be made between those who harm only themselves and those who corrupt or seduce others. Meanwhile it would be better if magistrates and judges recognized that there are many people who would like to fall in love with a girl, to marry and have children, to live and work in a socially approved way, but, for various reasons beyond their conscious control, these people are quite unable to do so.

THE ATTITUDE OF SOCIETY

CHAPTER XV

OTHER CIVILIZATIONS

The law is not the only control over our sexual behaviour. Indeed it is only the instrument of a more compelling control. In a well-organized community, the law should reflect the attitude of the society. This attitude is built up from our history, from the experiences of our forefathers, from the patterns set in the homes and in the schools, and from the ideas and prejudices of our neighbours. It is an infinitely complex thing and not altogether rational because, quite often, the avowed code is different from the actual behaviour.

We tend to think that our social attitude is the only possible one, that anything that deviates from our social code is wrong. But Western civilization, however superior it may seem to be, is only one of many alternatives. Only 25 per cent. of the world's population can be included in the nations that we think of as comprising Western civilization.

Other lands and other civilizations have quite different ideas. What is a sexual perversion in one community is considered quite normal in others. "Right" and "wrong" become meaningless when we compare one civilization with another. While we are sure some things are "right" and others are "wrong", primitive people seem to be more sophisticated in this respect than we are. Just as they know that the gods and the food habits of the next tribe differ from those of their own tribe, so they know that the sexual activities which they regard as natural differ from the natural sex customs of their neighbours.

Charles Darwin[11] pointed out that the hatred of sexual immorality and of sexual perversions is a "modern virtue" and entirely foreign in the nature of primitive tribes. On the island of Ponape in the Carolines, all the men on the island have only one testicle because all the boys at the age of seven or eight have the left testicle removed by a piece of sharpened bamboo. This is supposed to make the men more desirable to the women! This custom is just as much a part of their inherited tradition as our own sex mores are a part of ours.

The Arabs have their female harems and boys brothels; the

97

Indians have a textbook on (what we would call) perversions. Among the Masai,[23] circumcision is effected in such a manner that a portion of the skin is left behind to form a kind of button at the end of the penis. No woman will look at a man until the operation has been performed. It is not degeneration but simply a matter of custom.

Though our sex code has never permitted any kind of sexual relations between men, other civilizations have been more tolerant. Mackwood[53] quotes an example of this among a head-hunting tribe in New Guinea. "One adolescent male, of his own volition, donned a grass skirt instead of a loin cloth and took his place among the women making pottery. When his companions tried to lure him off on a head-hunting foray, Kama wouldn't go. They thought him a peculiar fellow, but as it was no business of theirs they shrugged their shoulders and left him to it. In a year or so Kama married and begat a family, and kept on with his pottery-making. No one ever called him a "cissie" or made him feel inferior—metaphorically castrated and anxiously robbed of power and the emotional security of social approval—and so he was able naturally to fulfil his biological sexual function, and had his secure place in society."

Devereux[12] found a striking example of institutionalized homosexuality. The Mohave Indians are a strong, virile and adventuresome race, but when they are not engaged in fighting or avenging some wrong, they have a remarkably kind and sunny disposition. Apart from procreation, they have a completely humorous attitude towards sex. There are only two important ceremonies—one when a child is born, and the other is the initiation of an *alyha*.

If it appeared that a young Indian boy was not interested in the virile masculine pursuits and that he would not fit into the aggressive life that an Indian brave was supposed to lead, his parents would arrange an initiation ceremony. After this initiation, the boy would formally be proclaimed an *alyha* and assumed a name befitting a person of the opposite sex. Once the ceremony was over, the *alyha* resented being called by his former masculine name. Not that this was particularly unusual in Mohave society, for they all used to change their names whenever they got tired of the old ones and resented being called by their discarded names. Word was sent to various settlements, inviting people to attend an "accustoming" feast. They wanted them to get used to the idea of seeing the boy in a woman's dress. Similar "accustoming" feasts were also held when someone lost an eye.

An *alyha* was not teased by the others. The Mohave consider that the *alyha* cannot help his temperamental disposition and so

98

they treat him as if he were a woman. Eventually he would marry one of the Indian braves. Devereux gives us an account of the curious homelife of the *alyha*:

Alyha were not courted like ordinary girls. The man did not go to the *alyha's* house or to the house of his parents and sleep beside him in chastity for a night or two before leading him away to his home. (This was the custom for courting girls.) It is not impossible however that for the sake of creating a comical situation, a thing paramount in the Mohave pursuit of sexual pleasure, on occasion a man went through the habitual courtship for an *alyha* because it appealed to his sense of the preposterous.

Once they were married the *alyha* made exceptionally industrious wives. The certitude of a well-kept home may have induced many a Mohave to set up house with an *alyha*.

After some months of married life, the *alyha* usually went through a hypothetical pregnancy. They observed the customary pregnancy taboos as rigidly or even more so than the normal women, conforming to many obsolete customs even, and compelling their husbands to observe their share of taboos, as befits expectant fathers. This gave rise to never ending jests at the expense of the husbands. The *alyha* stuffed rags and bark under their skirts, in increasing quantities, to make their abdomens protrude. In due time they make a decoction of mesquite beans which is said to cause severe constipation.

Eventually they had severe abdominal pains for a day or two, which they dubbed labour-pains. When the faeces could no longer be withheld the *alyha* retired into the bushes. After that they returned to the house and claimed to have given birth to a stillborn child. People would hear the *alyha* wailing and mourning for the imaginary child. They clipped their hair and compelled their husbands to clip their hair in the fashion befitting mourners.

Divorcing an *alyha* was not an easy matter. "They are so strong they might beat you up," the husbands complained. Some men who had enough of it tried to get rid of them politely, alleging barrenness of the *alyha*. But no *alyha* would admit such a thing. They would begin to fake pregnancy.

The husband of the *alyha* had to bear the brunt of the jokes that flew right and left in his presence but they seldom teased the *alyha* himself. "He was an *alyha*, he could not help it." But the husband of an *alyha* had no such excuse and was fair game to all and sundry.

Devereux's comments on the social aspects of this institutionalized homosexuality are revealing:

"Socially speaking Mohave civilization acted wisely perhaps in acknowledging the inevitable. This airing of the abnormal tendencies of certain individuals achieved several aims. It deprived certain modes of a typical behaviour of the glamour of secrecy and sin and of the aureola of persecution. It enabled certain persons swaying on the outskirts of homosexuality to obtain the desired experience and find their way back to the average tribal pattern without the humiliation of a moral Canossa. It created what is known as an 'abscess of fixation' and localized the disorder in a small area of the body social. Last of all the very publicity given to their status did not permit homosexuals to insinuate themselves into the confidence of normal persons under false colours and profit by some temporary unhappiness of the latter to sway them. They had to compete with the normal blatant sexuality not in the dark groves of Corydon and Sappho but in the open daylight, on the acknowledged playground of normal sexuality—at gatherings and feasts."

What is and what is not a perversion depends upon the civilization in which we live. Even in Western civilization the sex codes vary from country to country. The whipping that took place in English homes, in English schools and in English prisons until recently has been termed a peculiarly English perversion by other European countries. The connection between sex and the cane has been known to psychologists for some time. It is not unusual for a whipping to produce an erection in a schoolboy and frequent repetition of active or passive flagellation can assume an overwhelming attraction. Dr. Keale, Headmaster of Westminster School from 1809 to 1834, was so well known for his frequent beatings that it was said that "he knew the posteriors of his pupils better than their faces". There is no doubt that beating can become a sexual perversion and there may be some connection with this and the way the use of the cane is handed down from one generation to another as almost a sacred tradition in some English families and public schools.

It is probably unfair to speak of flagellation as an English perversion even fifty years ago, but it is an example of how one nation can brand the activities of another nation as perverse because they are not identical with its own. This country has led the world in developing a system of democracy, in discovering and developing the resources of the earth, and in many other ways. But it would be a mistake to assume that all our ideas and customs are right and anyone else's are wrong.

The ancient Greeks from whom we inherited the first ideas of democracy had a very different sex code from our own. Homosexuality was encouraged and fitted into the pattern of their civilization. It provided a means of education for cultural purposes in Athens, and it was part of the military system in

Sparta. This wide sex freedom did not prevent the highly civilized Greeks giving the world a rich heritage in art and learning.

In other civilizations, homosexuals have been considered valuable for their specific gifts of art, insight and ordered skill, but such practices have never been tolerated in this country. Throughout our history, the record shows that homosexuals have been punished with the severest penalties and persecuted with the utmost cruelty. The record also shows that this behaviour occurs in every century and under every régime. An instinct so deeply rooted in the nature of some men cannot be forcibly suppressed. It appears in every generation and in every class of society. Many men who were prominent in English history have been homosexual, including at least four Kings of England.

The Normans who settled in England after the conquest were known to have had a number of homosexuals among them. "The gilded youth of Norman England began to wear long garments like women and let their hair grow long."[62] Of William II, Edward Freeman[26] wrote: "Into the details of the private life of Rufus it is well not to grope too narrowly; in him England might see on her own soil habits of the ancient Greek and the modern Turk."

The homosexual activities of Edward II resulted in his murder in 1327. According to Higden,[37] "He was sleyne with a hoote broche putte thro the secret place posteriale".

Nicholas Udall was a teacher at Eton when he wrote *Ralph Roister Doister*, the first comedy written in the English language. In 1541 he was accused of a homosexual offence and convicted. After he had served his sentence, he was appointed Vicar of Bramtree and Director of Westminster School. Marlowe, the contemporary playwright of Shakespeare, wrote: "All thei that love not tabacco and boyes are fooles." Francis Bacon wrote an essay on beauty that does not mention the female body. His homosexual activities became so well known that his mother remonstrated with him.

The advent of the reign of James I produced the well-known saying: "*Rex fuit Elizabeth, nunc est regina Jacobus.*" Robert Carr, who had progressed from page-boy to the Earldom of Somerset under the patronage of James I, threatened to reveal publicly that "the King has slept with him" when he was put on trial for murder.

According to an English document of 1643,[6] the Vicar of Arlington declared that he "preferred men to women as regards sexual intercourse because of the shame and dishonour that might arise from begetting bastards." The Duchess of Orleans wrote of William III: "The King is said to have been in love with Albermarle as with a woman, and they say he used to kiss his hands before all the Court."[70] Edward Ward in his history of London clubs[73] mentions Mollie's Club in which the members were "so totally destitute of masculine attributes that they prefer to behave like women".

In 1810, the innkeeper of the White Swan in Vere Street was tried for allowing his house to be used for immoral purposes. In the hope of obtaining a milder sentence, he offered to give the names of the rich and distinguished visitors to his house, but this further incensed the judge and he was sentenced to the pillory. Had the judge availed himself of the innkeeper's offer, many well known and distinguished men would have been compromised for "even men in priest's attire went straight from the chancel to that sink of iniquity in Vere Street and other similar places". This quotation is from a book entitled *The Phoenix of Sodom, being an Exhibition of the Gambols Practised by the Ancient Lechers of Sodom and Gomorrah, embellished and improved with the Modern Refinements in Sodomitical Practices by the members of the Vere Street Coterie of detestable memory*—by Holloway (1813).

The Yokel's Preceptor was published in 1850[79] as a guide to the innocent visiting London. The unknown author warns that "Poofs have increased in the capital . . . not so very long ago signs and bills were hung in the windows of respectable hotels in the vicinity of Charing Cross with the notice: Beware of Paederasts."

In Victorian England, all forms of sex were considered shameful; this does not decrease the incidence but merely drives the behaviour underground. An Italian visitor was told: "My friend, you must give up the habit of kissing one of your own sex; it is not the custom in England and is only done by women."[13] This advice would still apply to-day, but it is in marked contrast to the behaviour of the gentleman in the early part of the nineteenth century whose foppish dress and habits are well known. The trials of Oscar Wilde were not the only evidence of homosexuality at this period. The Holborn Casino, the Argyll Rooms and the auditorium of the Empire Theatre were all well-known meeting-places for the men who wore green carnations. W. T. Stead[68] in the *Review of Reviews* in 1895 wrote: "Should everyone found guilty of Oscar Wilde's crime be imprisoned, there would be a very surprising emigration from Eton, Harrow, Rugby and Winchester to the jails of Pentonville and Holloway."

All through history, the homosexuals have contributed to the art and culture of our civilization. Nor have they been found to be lacking in courage, in statesmanship or in warfare. Many great reformers, distinguished statesmen and brave soldiers, including

Frederick the Great who possessed all three of these qualities, have had homosexual tendencies.

Some of the more famous have been mentioned, but, of course, there were many more who have not left their mark on history. Homosexuals like to claim that artists, actors, writers, etc., are better because of their abnormality.

They believe that they possess a sensitivity and an artistic insight that is denied the ordinary man. But it is more likely that these homosexuals who achieved greatness did so not because of their abnormality, but notwithstanding it. In spite of the fact that they were forced to conduct their emotional life in secret, or were hounded by society, they managed to turn out fine work. These were the truly great men who managed to rise above a difficult emotional handicap. There are many more who could add to the general happiness of mankind if society would help instead of hinder them as they try to overcome this handicap.

CHAPTER XVI

PUBLIC OPINION TO-DAY

THE BRITISH VIEW homosexuality with the same moral horror to-day as they always have. The attitude has hardly changed in hundreds of years. It is considered to be something so degraded that even its existence is only acknowledged in the form of pornographic humour or disgusted scorn. A candid discussion on it and serious thought on what is to be done about it, is unthinkable in ordinary society. The amount of prejudice and extreme emotional reaction engendered by the very word is remarkable.

Such is the silence and mystery that surrounds the whole subject that it is no wonder that, when they are forced to think about it, most people are guided by untutored superstitions rather than the facts. To these people a homosexual person is someone who deliberately, perversely, and of his own free will, flouts all the laws of God and man in order to indulge himself in debauchery; men who practise this wicked vice deserve no sympathy and get none. Yet only a brief examination of the causes has shown that it is a sickness of the mind beyond the control of most homosexuals. Even those who are prepared to admit that it is a disease feel that it is merely a matter of a little self-control. This is just a pious belief that will not stand up to investigation. But so widespread is this belief that a number of homosexuals have married because they felt certain that they could control these tendencies. More often than not the results have been tragic.

The attitude of the Church has been inherited from the old Jewish sex code with their horror of any kind of sex that does not lead to reproduction. Yet some of the greatest spiritual leaders have preached complete abstinence which, from the biological point of view, is no more constructive. Christian beliefs are supposed to be based upon the Bible but it is difficult to find the authority for many of the rigid sex prohibitions endorsed by the Church. Some ministers of religion seem to take little account of the power of the sex drives. It is not generally realized that man is one of the most highly sexed of all animals, but the Church tends to regard sex as a mechanical, easily controlled process and any sign of deviation from the set standard is a heinous sin.

Jokes about "pansies" are made by men who would not dream of making a jest at the expense of a man with a glass eye or a serious disease. On the radio and in the theatres the "queer gags" always get a laugh, yet in a theatre seating 2,000 men and women, over fifty will probably have strong homosexual tendencies. This kind of attack by ridicule upon things unpopular or misunderstood is very easy and helps to relieve any possible guilt feeling.

There is no point in mentioning all the ways the homosexual is made the subject of laughter, scorn and persecution in our present-day society; for those who understand the strange workings of the subconscious mind, the reason is not hard to find. For homosexuality arouses not only passion and prejudice but also reactions of a more profound and intractable nature.

It is an accepted psychological fact that a strong impulse in the unconscious may be disguised by means of a special defence mechanism called "projection". It is a mental process which enables impulses belonging to the individual to be attributed to persons in the outer environment and so treated as external. One of the great disadvantages of projection is that it deprives him of insight into his own mechanism. Thus a man with a homosexual predisposition may unconsciously find mental relief by projecting his own tendencies upon someone else.

An important characteristic may also be masked by its opposite in the conscious mind. A tendency to alcoholism may be replaced by a fanatical attitude towards temperance; the desire to excel at games and the awareness of some physical disability may be closely allied in origin; a talkative and bombastic disposition may hide a gnawing feeling of inferiority in the unconscious; and an aggressive, vitriolic attitude to homosexuality may be a defence against these tendencies.

Due to early influences beyond their control, hundreds of thousands of men have marked homosexual tendencies in their make-up. The violence of their denunciation represents a desperate repudiation of their own homosexual tendencies. It is impossible for these people to approach the problem of homosexuality with any kind of emotional detachment. Many of these people are as badly in need of psychological treatment as the homosexuals they so violently condemn.

The symptoms can sometimes be seen in men with a morbid fear of physical contact with their own sex. The men who find the hand on the arm or across the shoulder to be repellent, who cannot bear to hold another man on the lap in a crowded car, or who avoid sleeping in the same room with another man. Moralistic indignation and an urge to punish are signs of a projected homosexual tendency. It is a defence mechanism, to be found in all of us, which takes the form of a hostile disapproval of an activity which we would like to carry out ourselves.

Hence the homosexual finds himself endangered and repulsed by the other people in the community. His sexual outlet—his only sexual outlet, for any other would be repulsive to him—is regarded as a criminal, moral, religious and social offence. He is forced to conceal his way of living and to try and mislead his neighbours as to the truth. If he is to follow his natural instincts, he is condemned to live in a world of secrecy and shame.

What is the result of this attitude of the community? It does not change the homosexual into a heterosexual. It does not solve any of the problems or make anyone's life easier. It may drive the homosexual into seduction. Most homosexuals would prefer an adult partner, but if he misjudges his choice, he will get scorn, moral indignation, or even a punch on the nose; instead he may be tempted to seduce a boy because he knows the chances of success are greater and the results of failure not so likely to become the subject of a story in the local tavern.

It seems almost as if society as a whole has the same guilt feeling towards homosexuality as some individuals possess. Society created the homosexual and, as a defence measure against admitting this unsavoury truth, it seeks to stamp it out by ruthless persecution.

The effects of projection can be seen clearly in the less complex Iatmul civilization of the Middle Sepik River.[55] The Iatmul boys are brought up by their mothers away from their fathers and surrounded by a completely feminine environment. At puberty they go through an initiation ceremony and from then on they are supposed to be tough, aggressive and intolerant of anything approaching femininity. But their childhood experiences in feminine surroundings have not prepared them for this sudden change and many of the boys are unable to develop the masculine attributes which tribal custom demands. It seems as if the Iatmul culture, consciously or unconsciously, recognizes this weakness and the whole life of an Iatmul man is riddled with taboos as a defence against the strong homosexual inclinations of nearly all the males. The slightest sign of effeminacy is regarded as weakness, and men walk about often comically carrying their small wooden stools fixed firmly against their buttocks.

The upbringing of the child in Britain is not so distorted, nor are the sex taboos so meaningless, but the same situation is present. Perhaps the boy grows up over-protected by his mother;

106

his father does not return from work until the child is in bed and he goes fishing on Sundays and so hardly ever plays with his child for long periods; the boy moulds himself on his mother and already the first tendencies are instilled; he goes to a boarding school or joins an all male youth club and by intuition, luck or illicit experience he gets the wrong ideas about sex; he is not encouraged to marry until he can support a wife, so he has no legitimate sexual outlet when his sexual impulses are most violent and urgent. Not all family histories are like this—it may not even be typical—but enough of these things happen sufficiently often to turn a large number of men towards homosexuality.

Then when society discovers that a young man has a homosexual tendency, he is driven out of the town, given no chance to meet any girls and forced to join the society of other homosexual outcasts, thereby reinforcing his tendency.

Public opinion has always lagged at least 100 years behind medical knowledge as regards sex. Only fifty years ago, the publisher of Havelock Ellis' *Studies in the Psychology of Sex* was arrested and accused "of having unlawfully and wickedly published and sold, and caused to be procured and to be sold, a wicked, bawdy, and scandalous, and obscene book . . . intending to vitiate and corrupt the morals of the liege subjects of our Lady the Queen, to debauch and poison the minds of divers of the liege subjects of our said Lady the Queen, and to raise and create in them lustful desires, and to bring the liege subjects into a state of wickedness, lewdness, and debauchery".[18]

The sex code should be the translation of social needs into a series of rules, some written, some a matter of tradition. The new medical and psychological discoveries of the last fifty years have changed our social needs, but the sex code has remained as before, producing a continual disparity between our lives and our rules.

People regard our sex code as something that cannot be changed because it is "right" and something that is morally "right" cannot be altered or brought up to date. Yet it is impossible to find any divine inspiration, or even common sense, in our sex code. William Brend[8] in his book *Sacrifice to Attis*, points out that the sex code is different even in the neighbouring countries of Europe:

"The sex code varies, and has varied in almost every respect, and it is impossible to find any consistent principle which has served as its basis. In one country polygamy is permitted, in another it is a crime. Abortion is punished in England but performed by the State in Russia. Homosexuality is an offence in some countries, but not in others; in this country it is an offence in men but not in women. Books may be bought freely in Paris which are banned in London; on the other hand the sale of contraceptives is allowed in England but forbidden in France."

Brend points out that the ethical code is common to all European countries, but "It is quite possible to observe the ethical code and infringe the local sex code. A man or woman may be homosexual and yet display all the virtues of kindliness and self sacrifice."

Our social attitude to homosexuality can and should be changed but first the people of this country will have to learn more about the problems involved. All the finest medical and legal minds in this country agree that the present attitude of the public is harsh and vindictive. This attitude is often a complex—a reflection of a person's own homosexual component. It will be impossible to change this attitude until it is realized that all of us are balanced somewhere between the two poles of heterosexuality and homosexuality and millions of our fellow men have this homosexual tendency to a greater or less extent

Section VI

LEVELS OF HOMOSEXUAL SOCIETY

CHAPTER XVII

PERVERSIONS

Homosexuals are to be found throughout the entire physical range of the population, from the virile, manly sportsman to the mincing, lisping butterfly. On one end of this scale are footballers, boxers, strong, muscular labourers and tough, energetic businessmen. On the other end are slim, soft-skinned, high-voiced pansies who are indistinguishable from women when wearing female clothes. The frequency of overt sexual activity is equally varied. There are some men who are very definitely homosexual and yet have never had an overt experience; there are others who have seven or more experiences each week. It by no means follows that the more recognizable homosexuals have the highest frequency. Many of the virile type are promiscuous; many of the effeminate type are inexperienced. There seems to be no correlation between the appearance and the frequency of sexual intercourse.

Equally varied are the methods of obtaining sexual satisfaction. Some clinical workers believe that homosexuality and perversions are inextricably mixed. This is true only in so far as homosexuality itself may be considered a perversion. Most of the investigations into methods of obtaining sexual satisfaction have been made in prisons or clinics. As these groups contain a number of the dregs of society, the amount of perversion is large but it is doubtful whether it would be much more than the amount of perversion found in a similar group of heterosexuals. Krafft-Ebing[47] has said that sadism, masochism and fetishism are relatively more common in heterosexuals, and that in over-sexed cases the heterosexuals are apt to be more depraved than the homosexuals.

By far the most common method of obtaining orgasm is by mutual masturbation. This is usually the climax to kissing, passionate love-making and more sexual play than is common with man and woman. It is unwise to make too wide a generalization, but in the main it can be said that homosexuals indulge in more sex play, holding each other very tight and working up to a high pitch of excitement until the orgasm comes with only the minimum amount of manipulation.

The second most common method is intracrural intercourse in which much the same procedure as in mutual masturbation takes place with one partner on top of the other.

The third most common form is anal intercourse. Many people assume that this is the only method of overt sexuality that exists between homosexuals but this is not the case. Hirschfeld[38] estimated that less than 8 per cent. indulged in this form of behaviour in Germany, but there is evidence to suggest that the frequency is higher in this country; nevertheless it is not so common as the layman is apt to suppose. It is not, of course, unknown between men and women. Clifford Allen[2] points out that "the nerve supply of the sexual organs, as well as the anus, is derived from the embryological cloaca so that analism is not so biologically outrageous as it appears at first sight". Among some primitive tribes,[12] the proper way to prepare a virgin girl for heterosexual experience is to first practise anal intercourse on her for a few weeks.

Anal intercourse between homosexuals seems to be largely a matter of conditioning. If the first experience of the passive partner is painful, it is probable that he will not allow anal intercourse to be performed on him in the future. There are many of the feminine-looking homosexuals who will not tolerate anything of this kind. On the other hand there are others in whom the erotic zone seems to have been wholly transferred from the genitals to the anus; these people will not allow the active partner to touch the genitals and they experience ejaculation only at the climax of anal intercourse. One case of analism reported by Williams[77] stated that he never had any desire to masturbate and he "loses his passion if his lover touches his genitalia".

This complete transfer of the erotic zone is often caused by faulty training during elimination learning and is extremely difficult, if not impossible, to cure. There is one other factor which encourages the practice of analism which is more psychological than physical. In some love affairs between two men, one partner is extremely anxious to play the part of the wife as completely as possible; he will do the cooking, the laundry, look after the home and, though this does not follow inevitably, he may wish to act the part of the wife during sexual intercourse.

The division between active and passive homosexuals* is not

* There is often confusion about the terms "active" and "passive". At times they are used to indicate aggressiveness or receptivity in the role of soliciting or making advances. But it does not always follow that the man who makes the advances plays the active role in the sexual act. In this book the term "active" indicates the masculine role in fellatio or anal intercourse, and "passive" indicates the feminine role in fellatio or anal intercourse.

so marked as is commonly supposed. Many prefer either an active or passive role but it is not always an exclusive practice and sometimes the preference changes in later life. Kinsey found that out of 108 passive homosexuals, fifty-five (51 per cent.) had later made distinctly successful heterosexual adjustments.

Perhaps it had better be pointed out at this stage that pseudo-homosexuals almost always restrict their homosexual activities to sodomy, possibly because it is closest to the normal hetero-sexual act. Loeser[51] studied 270 cases sent to an American Army hospital. Of the sixty cases diagnosed as "no disease" and not considered true homosexuals, all were found to be under court-martial charges for sodomy. Only twenty-five of the 210 true homosexuals had been tried by general court martial for sodomy.

These pseudo-homosexuals function on either heterosexual or homosexual levels, depending upon circumstances and surroundings. They are essentially sexual psychopaths and their one object is to achieve sexual orgasm in the easiest and most available manner. Whether this primary goal of orgasm is achieved with a woman or a man is of little importance to these people. Psychiatrists have little difficulty in separating the pseudo-homosexuals from the true homosexuals. The etiology of pseudo-homosexuality is quite distinct and, together with other psychopathic sex offences, is beyond the scope of this book.

Kinsey found a large incidence of fellatio (coitus in os) in the United States but it is doubtful if it is as common in this country. There are, however, some cases where this is the exclusive practice and the active partner ejaculates during intercourse (taking the penis orally) without any manipulation of his own penis.

Sadism and masochism occur among homosexuals but not so often as between men and women. A common factor in this perversion among men is the discovery by a schoolboy that he gets a measure of sexual excitement, and sometimes an erection, from a beating. Other sadistic practices such as tieing up and rituals involving excretory defilement are very rare among homosexuals because there is seldom a dominant partner in an affair. There have also been very occasional homosexual murders, either premeditated or as a result of sadistic behaviour. Exhibitionism, fetishism and scopophilio (peeping Toms) are also found among homosexuals but are less frequent than among heterosexuals.

It has already been pointed out that what is considered a perversion in one civilization is part of the custom and culture of another. Even within our own civilization it is difficult to make an arbitrary distinction. The young man on the beach displaying his muscles in the briefest swim trunks is not very far from exhibition-ism; the only slightly disguised delight that some schoolmasters and parents take in corporal punishment seems to be very near a form of sadism. Even when only the perversions with definite anti-social results are considered, it is difficult to estimate how much of it is to be found among homosexuals. Although it is far from true that perversions are always to be found with homo-sexuality, it is probable that they are slightly more prevalent than in heterosexuals. There is one minor and one major reason for this.

The minor reason has already been mentioned while discussing analism. Some homosexuals take their relationship so seriously that they go through a form of "marriage", give the partner a ring and refer to each other as husband and wife. Although this is regarded as a subject for ribaldry outside their immediate circle of friends, the "wife" often attempts to play his part to the limit of his physical capabilities. Such people often display many of the qualities of the female sex, such as tenderness, neatness, sympathy and a wifely solicitude for the other partner; it can be said that they make excellent "wives" in every way except one, and they attempt to get over this physical deficiency by playing the passive part in anal intercourse.

Only a few go so far as to attempt to form this definite husband-wife relationship, but the other reason for the spread of perversion applies to all homosexuals, and affects all but the best. The continual persecution and unrelenting scorn of society towards this abnormality produces an attitude of mind in the homosexual which is harmful and sometimes crippling. When he realizes that he is doomed to become either the butt of the people around him, or else for ever hide his emotional life away from them, in time he will begin to despise the moral laws of this society that has so unreasonably put him in the social pillory. He gets the idea that either society will break him or he must break society.

In the extreme form the man broken by society will suffer from serious mental disturbances which on the surface will seem to have little connection with his homosexual difficulties. The man determined to break society will be involved in all kinds of psychopathic crimes; these may seem to have no outward connection with his homosexuality, but a number of seemingly unrelated crimes are often found to have a homosexual origin.

That is the position at its worst, but the persecution by the rest of society has its effect on nearly all homosexuals to a lesser extent. It begins in a simple enough way with a feeling that as the com-munity is against him, why respect the community's customs and traditions. So he will wear unusual clothes, show little regard for everyday manners and etiquette, hold unusual beliefs or descend into a kind of apathetic anarchism. If the homosexual does not guard against this condition of mind, he will find that most of his thinking will become anti-social. This may result in an overall persecution complex and a tendency to blame other people for his own faults and failures; sometimes it results in out-and-out anti-social behaviour either in his occupation or during his leisure—an unconscious desire to harm or get even with his oppressors; very occasionally it results in intense concentration upon work in an attempt to shut out the rest of society, so producing a genius or a fanatic according to the success or failure of the venture.

The implications of this attitude are very wide indeed. It produces a strong inclination to reject the approved patterns of society and especially in matters connected with sex. Hence the homosexual is more apt to try other methods of obtaining sexual satisfaction which may lead to the development of perversions.

Sometimes a heterosexual perversion can be found to have a homosexual origin. When a man is not easily aroused by a woman, he may find it necessary to practise some kind of sadism (beatings, rituals, biting and drawing blood) before he can reach a climax. From the point of view of society, it might have been better if such a man had developed as an overt but harmless homosexual rather than as a man who must inflict pain and distress upon his wife before he can obtain sexual satisfaction. It is also certain that a large number of the infanto-homosexual and infanto-heterosexual seductions are the result of repressed homosexual tendencies which would have been relatively harmless if they had been guided and controlled by psychotherapy.

CHAPTER XVIII

PROSTITUTION

Most of the homosexuals who practise the extreme forms of perversion resort to male prostitutes to find sexual satisfaction. This is because each perversion tends to become exclusive until it becomes the only way in which the subject can be sexually aroused. Thus the sadist is not interested in other homosexual activities and other homosexuals avoid the sadist. The pervert can only be sure of finding an accommodating partner when he pays an experienced male prostitute who is not concerned with sexual arousal but merely with satisfying the "customer". Many of the male prostitutes are heterosexual and only take part in homosexual relations as a way of making easy money. They are often completely depraved and are prepared to perform any perversion if it will increase their reward.

The attitudes of prostitutes of both sexes are very similar. They get no pleasure out of sexual activities and the whole matter of sex is measured in terms of goods and money. It is of little importance to them whether their original tendencies were homosexual or heterosexual because they have lost any feelings that they may have had at one time. They despise the people who pay for the lease of their bodies and do not enjoy sexual relations outside their professional activities any more than a road-sweeper would enjoy sweeping the road without payment. The following case is not altogether typical because the subject gave some thought for the future which is unusual in most prostitutes. He is now 35 years old, married and in gainful employment. He did not appear to be very ashamed of his past history although he was anxious that his employer should not find out about it.

Case XIII. "I started in a casual sort of way, just pocket-money stuff, until I was 18 when I came to London with the intention of making money on the streets. I don't ever remember getting much pleasure out of these jobs but you must remember that I would only go with old men who looked as if they had plenty of money. It wasn't as easy as I thought and I was forced to work through the day as well. I used to go out every night but I didn't always find a queer. I think this was because I was careful not to look too obvious. I didn't want to be picked up by the police before I made that fortune which I had been told was to be made on the streets. I only had one bit of trouble with the police and that was when we were in a barn off the Great West Road. A copper caught us right in the act. The queer gave the cop a couple of quid and disappeared. The cop asked me if I had any money. I had but I didn't let on, so he satisfied himself on me in the barn. At first I would do only masturbation but when one man offered me double if I allowed him to commit sodomy, I let him do it. It was all the same to me and from then on I would do anything, although, of course, I charged more for sodomy.

"The money still wasn't coming in fast enough for my liking. The trouble is that so many of these queers want to take you out to dinner and the theatre and give you a good time, but I wasn't interested in that. I just wanted the cash. I realize now that I would have done better if I had gone for a lower-class trade. There is more money in this up the stairs and out again quick than spending the night in some expensive flat. One day a young kid offered me a pound if I would commit sodomy on him. From then on I played both ends of the trade and was quite surprised at the number of rich young men who would pay for an active partner. I was going out with a girl at this time. She knew about me and didn't like it, but she liked the money I made. The funny thing is that she left me as soon as she found out I was playing the active part sometimes.

"Then I tried another idea. I knew lots of queers all over London but they get tired of you, you know. So I thought I'd make it my business to provide them with other pros. But this procuring didn't work too well. I found the queers and introduced them to the pros, but they're not a very honest lot, these pros, and they used to make off without paying me my rake-off. I would run into them later and they would swear that they never got a penny and they did it all for love but, of course, I knew better than that. I gave it all up when I joined the Army and I haven't bothered with it since. I sleep with the wife now when she wants it, but it doesn't interest me, men or women. I don't think I was ever queer. I just thought I could make a lot of money that way but it is not as easy as I thought."

The general public are inclined to think of male prostitutes as passive homosexuals, but there are a number who are exclusively active. These are mostly tall, well-built men who are prepared to play the active role with almost any man providing the price is right. They would resent being called "homosexual" and they rationalize that they are just "playing the queers". In fact there is a much stronger homosexual component in these men than in the full-time prostitutes who are devoid of any sexual feeling, and some of them end up by paying others to play the passive part. It is this group that often feels a strong compulsion to beat up the passive partner. This is not the same as sadism as it does not occur during the sexual activities but only after the climax has been reached; it is in the nature of an atonement for a strong guilt complex.

Two other groups who would indignantly deny the charge of prostitution should be classified under this heading. One group consists of the young men from the poorer sections of the community, who find they can drink in the best bars, sit in the most expensive seats at the theatre and generally enjoy a mode of existence that would otherwise be denied to them, if they can find a rich and willing partner. Many of these are not homosexual. Some of these manage to obtain these expensive pleasures and yet avoid overt homosexual activities by feeding the hopes of their patrons by promises of things to come. Others go through with the overt activities which they find unpleasant but worth while as an exchange for the bright lights and the gay life.

The second group of semi-prostitutes is made up of sailors and other Service-men who come to the larger towns on a week-end pass and save themselves the expense of paying for a room for the night. They spend the evening enjoying the pleasures of the town and then when the bars close, they come out on the streets to try to find someone who will put them up for the night. Some men are attracted by a uniform, particularly a sailor's uniform, and these Service-men do not have much difficulty in finding their board and lodgings. They are quite well aware of the fact that they will be expected to share one bed and as a rule they are prepared to do what is expected of them. Another type of prostitute is the "kept" man. He usually keeps to one partner for as long as he is prepared to shoulder the expenses. They are not to be found in the haunts frequented by the other prostitutes and only a connoisseur can detect the "*demi-monde* aroma".

Older prostitutes who no longer find it easy to get enough men to pay the rent often go in for robbery and blackmail. An example of robbery is provided by two sailors who had worked this racket several times before. The better-looking one who was used as bait got in conversation with a parson who was already under the influence of alcohol. While the parson was buying the drinks, the sailor managed to see enough of the contents of the priest's wallet to make it worth while proceeding with the plan. When he felt the parson was drunk enough, he made a suggestion to him and told him that he knew of a good place to go. The second sailor followed them and they both turned on the victim when they had led him into a dark street. On this occasion the parson was given back his wallet intact because one of the sailors got sudden qualms about robbing a minister of the Church. There is no question of homosexual practices in these cases. The only motive is robbery, using the homosexual tendencies of the victim as a means for accomplishing this end.

Blackmail is still frequent in London and other places. One group are highly skilled criminals who choose their victim with the utmost care and plan the scene and the compromising situation in great detail. They are so skilled at this operation that they can sometimes trap a normal man who has no homosexual intentions at all. Quite often the heterosexual will pay rather than be involved in unfavourable publicity and risk the unjustified disapproval of society. The other group consists of men who start an association with other men and then realize that a situation has arisen that can be used to extract more money out of them.

The law as it stands to-day is particularly favourable to blackmail. Whether they have actually indulged in homosexual intercourse or not, the fact that they have been alone in a private room with another man is enough to persuade most socially established men to pay up. Only a small percentage of the blackmail cases get reported to the police, and this is only when the victim finds that he is being bled white and has no more to lose. Men who have served a prison sentence for a homosexual offence often turn into blackmailers. When they come out of prison, they are still as homosexual as they ever were, but in addition they now have a grievance and a grudge against society in general. The police make a great effort to catch these criminals but their job is made doubly difficult by the secrecy and contempt which always surrounds homosexuality.

The problem of the male prostitute is as insoluble as that of the female. The method of dealing with the female prostitution merely aims at keeping it within bounds. The police know all the girls by their Christian names and every morning at Marlborough Street and Bow Street about a dozen girls pay their "licence fee" under Section 55 (11) of the Metropolitan Police Act of 1839. C. H. Rolph[63] reports this conversation with a prostitute:

" 'The police pick us all up in turn. It comes round about once a month. It's fair enough, really, it's only forty shillings. If you play the fool, get drunk or act saucy or something, you get it more often, and you've asked for it. I've no complaints about the coppers.' I asked her how she stood on the rota. She laughed. 'I was picked up this evening,' she said. 'You can see me at Marlborough Street Police Court in the morning, if you like.' Why did the police let her out again the same evening then? 'I've got to live, haven't I?' she said. 'They can't fine me forty bob if they don't let me earn it; they don't mind where it comes from so long as they get the money. They only keep you in the police station about twenty minutes. Charge you with "soliciting to the annoyance of passengers", and then let you go on bail. They know where we all live, you see, and they know we'll always turn up.' "

The police attitude to male prostitutes is quite different. There is no licensing system and no toleration of any sort. Male soliciting carries a penalty of six months' imprisonment, compared with the 40s. fine for women, and there is no necessity for the constable to "prove" that anyone was annoyed by the soliciting. The National Vigilance Society reports that West End convictions against "male persons persistently soliciting (or importuning) in a public place for immoral purposes" average about forty a month.

Female prostitution is on the decline in this country, mostly due to the greater use of contraceptives and more opportunities for intercourse between the sexes. Male prostitution continues much as it has done since the dawn of history. Most male prostitutes are young and in spite of the depths of depravity to which they have descended, many of them will respond to treatment. But it is an extremely difficult problem and we are a long way from finding the answer. It is certain, however, that a term of imprisonment without any attempt to reorientate the offender is not even a first step towards a solution.

CHAPTER XIX

STREET CORNERS

MANY OF THE PROSTITUTES and perverts are not homosexual in the strict sense of the word, but among them are a fair number of men with homosexual tendencies. It is convenient, therefore, to take this as the lowest strata of homosexual life. Above them, there seems to be four other levels with fairly sharp divisions between them, although men can move from one level to the next without much difficulty. These four levels might be named: (a) the street corners, (b) the queer bars, (c) the exclusive clubs, (d) the outsiders.

The street corner, as can be expected, is the most open homosexual society. It can easily be found—indeed, many normal people complain that it cannot be missed—and entry into the society can be made without formality. It consists of the prostitutes and other riff-raff mentioned in the previous chapter and, in addition, a number of other men also frequent these places. The two cases that follow are examples of the typical people to be found in these places.

Case XIV. J—— is 42, single, a buyer in a large departmental store, clean and well-dressed in appearance. He spends a lot of his off-duty hours prowling around these spots with the idea of meeting other men. He is somewhat cynical about life in general and is convinced that people who hang around these meeting places are "no good and not to be trusted, and that includes me". He refuses to go to the rooms of other men and as he lives with his married sister, it is impossible to take his partner back to his home. He is not prepared to pay prostitutes and seems to have developed some skill in avoiding other undesirables. When he meets a willing partner, no names or addresses are exchanged and his sexual activities are either performed in the park or in some back alley or, very occasionally, in a hotel room that he has taken in a false name. He cuts down the preliminaries as much as possible because "a queer's conversation is strictly limited". He is a confirmed "oncer" and has a strong guilt feeling after orgasm. He says that after he has had sexual experience with someone, he has a feeling of revulsion towards him and does not want to see him again. He believes that a measure of real affection is possible between two men but he has been let down so many times that he never allows himself to become attracted to anybody. What with the prostitutes, undesirables and his own attitude of distrust, it may take him three, four or more days before he finds a suitable partner. When he does, the whole episode is over in about thirty minutes. He says that he hurries away from his partner as soon after the climax as possible and the experience will settle him for three or four weeks. Then he feels the urge to prowl the streets again and he carries on with this same procedure about once a month.

There are a large number of homosexuals who have this embitterered and cynical attitude to their own abnormality. They seem to be able to see the futility of their present mode of living but they do not know how to get into a group that is more of their own cultural and intellectual level. As a result they consider all homosexuals to be worthless and include themselves in this condemnation.

It is sometimes assumed that the men who will never repeat a homosexual experience with the same partner are promiscuous because they are concerned only with the thrill of conquest, the variety of partners or the differences in sexual techniques. But it is more likely that these "oncers" suffer from a powerful guilt complex and any association with a previous experience is repugnant to them. It sometimes happens that this guilt feeling that follows a homosexual experience keeps a man away from these spots for a long period; when eventually he returns, the sight of a previous partner may revive the guilt feeling and he loses any desire to indulge in sexual activities and returns home.

The second case is about a man of 24. He was a clerical worker and seemed to be competent but not very interested in his work.

Case XV. "I think my family realized I was queer before I did. At any rate my father gave me a long lecture one day which seemed to consist mostly of long words and bad language. I didn't understand a word of it. I had a couple of schoolboy experiences but I didn't bother about them. When I was 17 I fell violently in love with a man about twenty years older. One day there was a whole crowd of us at a party and I kissed the back of his neck while he was playing the piano. He turned around and hit me in the face and there was the hell of an uproar. All the same he asked me to go camping with him a few weeks later and

122

we had sex together. We used to have sex together quite a lot after that, but he used to get angry if I showed any affection or tried to make love. He threw me over when I got drunk one evening and made another public scene. It has been much the same ever since. I've met lots of people who want to go to bed with me but I want to be loved and live with a person. I often hang around these places hoping I will meet someone nice. I've been lucky twice. One person I lived with for nearly two years. We split up when he started to get interested in someone else. If I had any sense I would have stuck around and tried to win him back, but I blew up and walked out on him. I've regretted it ever since. The other person was very nice and treated me just as if I was a girl. But he got fed up with all the dirty cracks made about us and he said he was going normal. I felt sure he couldn't but he told me I was a bad influence on him and so we split up. I've seen him around with another man since then but I don't think it was just an excuse to get rid of me. We were terribly in love at the time. They were both good mates and as I met them both here [an Underground station], I keep on coming back hoping I will be lucky a third time. But it's mostly rent [prostitutes] around here. I could never do anything like that, but I do allow men to pick me up and I talk to them for a time to see if I like them. I'm quite fussy, you know. Oh, they don't have to have a lot of money—I can get along on my own wages— but they've got to be clean, and nice, and show a bit of love. Most of them just want sex. If they suggest going to bed on the same night that I first meet them, then I can be pretty sure that it won't work out. Most of the people round here are dirt. They take you back with them and then when they've got what they want, they'll kick you out. They're just sex mad. You have to be awfully careful. The dicks [police] come down here and pretend to be queer themselves. But you never know. I may meet somebody nice some day."

This man has managed to keep some sort of standard up to the present. But the chances of finding a congenial partner are remote and as the intervals between finding a mate get longer and longer, he is likely to lower his standards and in time he may get as cynical as the "sex mad" people that he despises so much at present.

The people who frequent these places do so at great risk to themselves. They are the possible victims of police, blackmailers or robbers. But many of them say that they can distinguish between a genuine homosexual and the rest of the world. Many different theories are put forward to explain this ability to recognize these members of the same fraternity. Some people suggest that it is a matter of clothes. By this they do not mean that the clothes are necessarily effeminate, but homosexuals tend to take a greater interest in being neatly dressed and are usually ahead of the current fashion in men's wear. Sometimes this situation will delay an improvement in men's clothes; for many years it was not "done" to wear suède shoes because somehow they got the reputation of being "nancy-wear" and even now the stigma of homosexuality is promptly attached to any man who breaks out of conformity with his clothes.

There may be something in this theory. It is said that a woman appreciates neatness and clean linen in a man but new and startling innovations in a man's wear can look too much like competition. Long, long ago Ovid in his *Ars Amatoria* advised men who wished to please women to avoid feminine adorn- ments, and to leave these to the homosexual.[59] If it is true that men's clothes are usually chosen by their womenfolk, then the homosexual's clothes will have a subtle difference apparent to the women if not to the men. But it is precisely because the passive, effeminate type are easily recognized by their clothing that most homosexuals go out of their way to avoid anything that would associate them with this group. Those who claim that they can recognize a homosexual by his clothing, or by his effeminate mannerisms, walk or speech are probably only recognizing a certain type—the type who have been brought up with a strong feminine influence in their environment. There are many hundreds of others who have definite homosexual tendencies but have broad shoulders, large moustaches, or other very masculine attributes.

Others say that a practised observer can spot the homosexual by his eyes and general behaviour. He will show his awareness of men and a lack of it to women. There is no doubt that some men give themselves away when a good-looking young man enters a room, but this is not an infallible test. There are numerous heterosexual men who manage to cover up whatever sexual interest they may have in each pretty girl that they meet. As there is no physical difference between heterosexuals and homo- sexuals, it seems probable that there is no sure way of distinguish- ing them from outward appearances. But it is certain that most of the homosexuals can distinguish one another from the casual passers-by on these street corners.

Unlike the other homosexual levels to be considered later, the street corner is a loose social group. There are the prostitutes, racketeers, embittered "oncers" and those looking hopefully for an ideal partner. Anyone can join the group and, though they do not mix with each other, they are able to recognize one another. Homosexuals at other levels look down upon this heterogeneous group and they will never try to find a partner at this level; most of them are as repulsed by the sight as normal people and earnestly desire to have no connection with them. The inexperienced, the visitors from out of town and the desperate visit these places and, of course, they make ideal victims for the prostitutes, blackmailers and thieves.

CHAPTER XX

PUBLIC-HOUSES

ALTHOUGH THE "queer bars" are usually certain selected smoking-rooms and open to the general public, they make a surprisingly compact group. It is difficult to say why some taverns are selected and others not, but once they get the reputation their customers are almost entirely homosexuals. Locals avoid the place and if a visitor comes into that bar by mistake, he soon leaves no matter how attentive the publican may be. Not many of the tavern-owners complain if one of their bars get the reputation of being queer. It is good for business and the selected taverns nearly always have one or two other bars so that the normal public can be served undisturbed by the sight of the "pansies". Of course, the publican has to watch out that he does not get into trouble with the police; his customers can drop the mask of normality in these places but if he allows them to become too obvious, the police will raid the place and scare away his customers.

Most of the homosexuals who frequent these bars are careful not to get the publican into trouble with the police, for in a pathetic kind of way this place is their home. Some of them live with their families and most of them have to pretend to conform with the normal heterosexual code during working hours. It is only when they come here in the evening that they can "let their hair down" and feel at home. One seldom sees drunkenness in these bars because they do not come there to drink, but to meet other homosexuals, gossip about other people's affairs and talk about their own adventures. But the total consumption of alcohol during the week may be above average for it is a steady business; many of them go there every night.

There is seldom any public love-making, although there may be some furtive holding of hands underneath the table and a fair amount of flirting when a new member enters the group. No attempt is made to disguise their homosexuality and the visitor would have some difficulty with the jargon that they speak. For example, one might be heard to say: "I ran into Norman in a cottage and, of course, I sent her up about that.

She wasn't trading but I'm sure she's T.B.H." (I ran into Norman in a public lavatory and, of course, I teased him about being there. He wasn't looking for anyone but I'm sure he was open to offers.)

Boys are not tolerated in this group and the publican is careful not to serve anyone below the age of eighteen because he knows that the police keep a strict watch on these places. They nearly always come to these bars in pairs; but there is a subtle difference between pairs which would not be apparent to the visitor but is well known by all the regulars. Some of the pairs go around together but they are just "sisters". By that they mean they are not interested in each other sexually and when one of them finds a partner, the other retires gracefully or, possibly, does his utmost to win the new partner away from his "sister". The other pairs who come in are "affairs", recognized and discussed at length by the rest of the group. The duration of these affairs may be weeks, months or even years, but the partners are not free from flirtations and invitations from the others. Everyone is fair game in this group and those who find themselves temporarily without a partner will make strenuous efforts to obtain one, even if it involves splitting up an affair of long standing.

It may seem difficult to understand why two men who are happy with each other will take the risk of going to these places where the whole atmosphere of the group will tend to drive them apart. The reason is that, unless they are living together, this is often the only place where they can be together, and both of them feel that they are immune to the advances of the others. This next case-history is very typical and illustrates a difficulty common to most homosexual affairs.

Case XVI. G—— is in his middle thirties, stocky, broad-shouldered and good-looking. He is an executive in a wholesale firm in a large provincial town and lives out of town with a retired father and a younger sister. He is very much in love with L——, who is 24, slight and effeminate, and works as a waiter in the same town. G—— is completely masculine in his manner-isms and his appearance, and no one would suspect that he was homosexual. L—— is an obvious homosexual. They have been meeting two or three times a week for eighteen months and they are both exhilarated by each other's company. G—— is very worried about what would happen to his job if the truth came out and this is the cause of the only friction between them. L—— wants G—— to leave his family to come and live with him, and he is jealous of the girls that G—— meets during his normal social life. G—— is jealous of the other men who soon spot L—— as a homosexual and accuses him of flirting with them. Apart from this, they get on extremely well together and earnestly wish to be together as much as possible. But they dare not be seen together around town and the queer bar is the only place where it is safe for them to meet. Occasionally they go away for the week-end together but this is the only time they have any overt sexual experience. At other times they have to be content with a hurried good-night kiss in some dark doorway. So far there is no sign of this affair breaking up.

Besides the economic ties, the presence of children and the expense of divorce which hold together many unhappy marriages among heterosexuals, there are other moral sanctions that make it unlikely that homosexual affairs will last for long. There are some outstanding exceptions but most affairs last only a few months. First of all there is the outward pressure of social disapproval and the risk of severe punishment if caught. If one of the partners occupies an important place in the community, he runs the constant risk of losing his place. He must take extra precautions to see that his friends and business associates do not find out about it.

Many people find it repugnant to have to live a secret life, and the necessary precautions and constraints reduce them to a nervous irritation where they long to be rid of this association; so the affair breaks up although it is obvious that the break achieves no useful purpose and both partners will probably be involved in other affairs before very long.

In addition to the outward pressures, there is this biting, hurtful inward pressure from the members of the group. When facing difficulties that menace the group from outside, homosexuals all show a remarkable solidarity. But within the group, every affair is subjected to any amount of gossip and innuendos. Among the older regulars of a queer bar, many will have had affairs with each other; it is not difficult to imagine the tone of the remarks which ex-partners make about a new affair.

Most of the affairs start with the most serious intention of being "the real thing". Both partners feel that they can really make a success of the association and really do their best to ignore the outer and inner pressures that seek to divide them. The end of these affairs are often painful to one or both partners and they are left in a hopeless frame of mind, occasionally bordering on the suicidal. But the "rebound effect" is as powerful in homosexuals as with heterosexuals and most of them find someone else in time and once more set out to find something like real happiness in a new affair, convinced that this time, it will be "the real thing".

Case XVII. J—— is a typical example of this. He is only 22 but he is now in his fourth affair. Three of his four partners all come from this one social group in one of the London bars. The fourth affair has every appearance of being a success, but they have been together only a few weeks and his past history makes it seem unlikely that it will last for long. Yet J—— is not promiscuous. He is attractive enough to be the subject of numerous advances and invitations in this bar but he has always maintained a faithful allegiance to his partner during the limited period of each affair. The end of these affairs do not come because J—— has fallen for some other person; it is usually some trivial matter which leads to a quarrel and the parting. If these affairs had been bound by the legal code, social approval and family ties, it is possible that J—— would have risen above the trivial incidents that led to the disintegration.

The end of the trail for these people is often pathetic. Many of them continue to come to the bar so that they can be among people they feel at home with, although they are too old to be able to find new partners. Some may have made enough money to "keep" a young man for a time. Others decide to give up all sexual activities and leave the homosexual scene, but by this time they are doomed to a lonely old age without families or friends.

CHAPTER XXI

EXCLUSIVE CLUBS

THE MOST EXCLUSIVE homosexual society is to be found in the private clubs in and around London. Membership to these clubs is very restricted and even a recommendation from a member is no guarantee that the application for membership will be accepted. On some nights in the week members may bring in guests, but they are expected to be careful about these invitations; the guests are expected to be in sympathy with the general ideas of the members and if after three or four visits they are not invited to join the club, it is generally understood that the guest is not considered suitable for membership. Only wealthy and successful men can afford to be members, while boys and youths are not allowed in the club rooms.

These people are the homosexuals who have adjusted themselves to their condition. Most of them have succeeded in keeping their emotional life far apart from their professional activities. Many of them are proud of their condition and regard themselves as superior to normal people.

It is not unusual for homosexuals of all levels to believe that they are intellectually above average. The assertion is not justified in most cases but in this group there is some substance to the claim. The clubs are expensive as well as exclusive, and it is argued that a man handicapped by an anti-social tendency has to have greater drive and ability to attain the same measure of success as a heterosexual who does not find it a burden to control his sexual life.

The persecution and scorn which a homosexual has to face forces him to think about his relations with the external world. As he has found one section of the decreed social morality to be impractical as far as he is concerned, he will be less likely to accept the other rules of society without question. In a small mind, this can lead to anti-social activities and anarchism. But in a man of high intellectual integrity, it produces a philosophical outlook which is not often found in a heterosexual. His deviation from the normal will force him to reflect about the world and about human existence. He will have to make a very real effort to fit himself into a society for which he is not emotionally fitted. If he succeeds, it is probable that in the process he will have acquired a certain intellectual profundity and a tolerant understanding of other men's difficulties.

The successful men who are members of these clubs come from many different professions and occupations. There are doctors, lawyers, accountants, business-men and stock-brokers. It is a mistake to think of homosexuals only as actors, artists and ballet dancers. While it is true that many of them are prominent in the artistic and entertainment fields, there are many others who possess as many differences in personality, character and mentality as do normal people. To the well-adjusted man, homosexuality is but one phase of his personality just as heterosexuality is but one phase of the personality of a normal man. Many of them are well-educated, cultured persons who are perfectly at ease in any society, and are capable of holding responsible, high-salaried positions in all walks of life.

Woman guests are allowed into most of the clubs on certain nights. It is wrong to assume that homosexuals are misogynists. Many of them enjoy the company of women and go to dances and mixed parties although they do not, and cannot, feel any sexual stimulation in the presence of a woman.

In this society, bi-sexuals are considered immoral. They argue that a true homosexual could not tolerate such practices and so a bi-sexual is one who is only concerned with sensuality, the sex of the love object being immaterial. This judgment is based upon the misconception that one is either a homosexual or not. In fact we have found that there is a heterosexual-homosexual balance and a man may be at any point along this scale. There are a number of men who are around the middle of the heterosexual-homosexual balance and, in addition, there are others with strong homosexual tendencies who have been forced into heterosexual intercourse for environmental and social reasons. A more detailed investigation on bi-sexuals would probably show that most of them have strong homosexual tendencies and their heterosexual activities are no more than their own unsuccessful attempts to conform with the customs of their society.

It is a mistake to think that because two men are homosexual they are automatically drawn together. Little or no public love-making will be seen in these clubs, not so much because there is a law against it but simply because it is regarded as bad manners in the same way as love-making between heterosexuals in public places is considered to be bad form. There is a certain amount of flirtation and there are still those who feel the challenge to break up an established affair, but for the most part, the objects of affection are defined within narrow limits for these men. The affairs tend to last longer in this group although few of them are permanent.

The affairs at this level compass the entire scale from pure Platonism to ardent sensuality. It is in this group that one most often finds the spiritual form of homosexuality in which sexual contact is on a basis of friendship rather than sexual excitement. Goethe[7] speaks of "the remarkable phenomenon of the love of men for each other. Let it be admitted that this love is seldom pushed to the highest degree of sensuality."

Incredible though it may seem to the ordinary man, these spiritual affairs can be touched with tenderness, and affection, and something like happiness. It is possible for the love between two men to be just as pure and on just as lofty a plane as it sometimes is between a man and a woman. Krafft-Ebing[46] wrote: "A further proof that contrary sexual sensation is not . . . necessarily a vicious self-surrender to the immoral, is to be found in the fact that all the noble activities of the heart which can be associated with heterosexual love can equally be associated with homosexual love in the form of noble-mindedness, self-sacrifice, philanthropy, artistic sense, poetic activity, etc., but also the passions and defects of love."

Case XVIII. D—— is a successful business-man who lives with H——, the editor of a trade paper. Both are in the early thirties and except in working hours, they are seldom apart. They both earn good salaries and they live in an expensive flat. It is furnished in excellent taste and they are extremely proud of their home and lavish their attention on it like young newlyweds. There is a certain amount of physical love between them but the most striking thing about them is their complete emotional harmony and the way they rejoice in each other's company. The editor described the sexual side of their love affair as "unimportant". Both of them have masculine physiques and neither of them take, or want to take, the part of the passive partner. They occasionally visit one of the London clubs together, but most evenings they are content to stay at home or entertain friends. Although they are careful to keep their relationship secret from their business associates, they have a number of heterosexual friends. They have known each other for over six years and they have lived together for four years. They cannot remember ever having a serious quarrel and there seems every chance that their partnership will continue. Originally their interests were far apart, but each has made a conscious effort to understand and appreciate the other's recreations and pastimes, with the result that this partnership has had the effect of broadening the outlook of both partners. The editor describes his partner as a "companion, lover and intimate friend—a triple combination that I've never found in an ordinary marriage".

This is almost a classic example of the true meaning of love and unfortunately it is a combination all too rarely found in either heterosexuals or homosexuals. But if there are not many like this, it is true that one often finds an ecstatic and exalted quality in homosexual affairs. Most of them break down under the pressure of social disapproval and absence of legal status, but then it is doubtful if there would be as many long-time relationships between heterosexuals if it involved transgressing social customs and engaging in an activity that had a certain amount of danger attached to it.

There is no doubt that a homosexual affair has a much better chance of continuing at this club level where it is possible to separate the occupational activities from the emotional and physical love. But there have been examples of this same exalted quality in love affairs between homosexuals at all levels. Alexander Berkman[5] gives an example of this at the very lowest level where something like true love existed between two criminals. He reported a conversation with a doctor serving a sixteen-year sentence for a bank robbery.

" 'Look at the fellows here from the various reform schools. Why, it's a disgrace. The boys who come from outside are decent fellows. But those kids from the reformatories . . . you can spot them by looking at them. They are worse than street prostitutes.'

"My friend is very bitter against the prison element variously known as the girls, Sallies, and punks who for gain traffic in sexual gratification. But he takes a broad view of the moral aspect of homosexuality; his denunciation is against the commerce in carnal desires. As a medical man, he is deeply interested in the manifestation of suppressed sex. A general medical practitioner, he had not come in personal contact with cases of homosexuality. He had heard of paederasty; but like the majority of his colleagues, he had neither understanding for nor sympathy with the sex practices he considered abnormal and vicious. In prison he was horrified at the perversion that frequently came under his observation. For two years the very thought of such matters filled him with disgust; he even refused to speak to the men and boys known to be homosexuals, unconditionally condemning them—'with my prejudices rather than my reason'.

" 'But as the months and years passed, my emotions manifested themselves. It was like a psychic awakening. The desire to love something was strong upon me. . . . Somehow the thought of women gradually faded from my mind. When I saw my wife, it was just like a dear friend. But I didn't feel towards her sexually. One day, as I was passing in the hall, I noticed a young boy. He had been in only a short time, and he was rosy-cheeked, with a smooth little face and sweet lips—he reminded me of a girl I used to court before I was married. After that I frequently surprised myself thinking of the lad. I felt no desire toward him, except just to know him and get friendly. I became acquainted with him, and when he heard I was a medical man, he would often call to consult me about the stomach trouble he suffered. The doctor here persisted in giving the poor kid salts and physics all the time. Well, Aleck, I could hardly believe it myself, but I grew so fond of the boy, I was miserable when a day passed without seeing him. I was rangeman, then, and he was assistant on a top tier. We often had opportunities to talk. I got him interested in literature, and advised him what to read, for he didn't know what to do with his time. He had a fine character, that boy, and he was bright and intelligent. At first it was only a liking for him, but it increased all the time, till I couldn't think of any woman. But don't misunderstand me, Aleck; it wasn't that I wanted a "kid". I swear to you the other youths had no attraction for me whatever; but this boy—his name was Floyd—he became so dear to me, why, I used to give him everything I could get. I had a friendly guard, and he'd bring me fruit and things. Sometimes I'd just die to eat it, but I always gave it to Floyd. And Aleck—you remember when I was down in the dungeon six days? Well, it was for the sake of that boy. He did something and I took the blame on myself. And the last time—they kept me chained up for nine days—I hit a fellow for abusing Floyd; he was small and couldn't defend himself. I did not realize it at the time, Aleck, but I know now that I was simply in love with the boy; wildly, madly in love.

" 'It came very gradually. For two years I loved him without the least taint of sex desire. It was the purest affection I ever felt in my life. It was all-absorbing and I would have sacrificed my life for him if he had asked it. But by degrees the psychic stage began to manifest all the expressions of love between the opposite sexes. I remember the first time he kissed me. It was early in the morning; only the rangemen were out, and I stole up to his cell to give him a delicacy. He put both arms between the bars, and pressed his lips to mine. Aleck, I tell you, never in my life had I experienced such bliss as at that moment. It's five years ago, but it thrills me every time I think of it. It came suddenly; I didn't expect it. It was entirely spontaneous; our eyes met, and it

134

seemed as if something drew us together. He told me he was very fond of me. From then on we became lovers. I used to neglect my work, and risk great danger to get a chance to kiss and embrace him. I grew terribly jealous too, though I had no cause; I passed through every phase of a passionate love. With this difference, though—I felt a touch of the old disgust at the thought of actual sex contact. That I didn't do. It seemed to me a desecration of the boy, and of my love for him. But after a while that feeling also wore off, and I desired sexual relation with him. He said he loved me enough to do even that for me, though he had never done it before. He hadn't been in any reformatory, you know. And yet, somehow I couldn't bring myself to do it; I loved the lad too much for it. Perhaps you will smile, Aleck, but it was real true love. When Floyd was unexpectedly transferred to the other block, I felt that I would be the happiest man if I could only touch his hand, or get one more kiss.' "

CHAPTER XXII

THE OUTSIDERS

The three levels of homosexual society that have been considered so far are all composed of men who, if not completely adjusted to their situation, at least have recognized it and given up any serious attempt to alter it. This does not mean that many of them are not anxious to obtain a release from their abnormality, but they cannot see how this can be done and, for better or worse, they have found other homosexuals who are in a similar position to themselves.

Except for the visitors and inexperienced who find the street-corner meeting-places when they come to the larger towns, most of the people at these levels have learnt to avoid trouble. They know there are plain-clothes detectives watching these places and they have learnt how to sort out the prostitutes and criminals. There is still a large element of danger in pursuing these activities, especially from blackmailers, but their chances of avoiding these perils are much better than for the final level of homosexual society which for purposes of classification will be called *the outsiders*.

This is by far the largest proportion of homosexuals and is not strictly a level of society, for it embraces all those with homosexual tendencies who are not found on the other three levels. Even among men with the strongest desire for homosexual relations, there are only a relatively few who know where to find them. They cannot afford to become members of the exclusive clubs. They do not know about the "queer bars", or do not dare to go into them alone even if they know where they are. If they live in the country there will be no well-known meeting-places, and if they live in any but the largest towns, they will not wish to be seen around the street corners that are too well known. In any case, many of them are horrified at the things they see on these street-corners and a visit to one of them sometimes comes as a psychological shock—they realize that the men they see around there are suffering from the same disability as themselves and they ask themselves if they, too, must stoop so low in order to gratify their sexual drive. Most of them leave the place filled with horror, alarmed to discover that their abnormality is associated with prostitution and other forms of depravity.

The man with strong tendencies who lives in a small village is in a very difficult position. The slightest sign, the merest interest in another man is liable to start a wave of gossip throughout the village. This does not mean that country folk are more aware of the problem of homosexuality than the townsmen, but any activity which is unusual is a subject of conversation in a small community. If a countryman is tempted to journey into the nearest town in search of a sexual outlet, his inexperience makes it more likely that he will only find trouble. These outsiders consist of all classes of people who go for months and even years at a stretch without an overt homosexual experience. This may seem all to the good as far as society is concerned, but the results of such abstinence are not as satisfactory as moralists would have us believe. Sex is not a matter of spectatorship. It is a situation in which the most passive person must play some part if he is to participate fully in life. Except in rare cases where the individual has obtained a measure of successful sublimation more by luck than good judgement, the man who tries to suppress his sexual drive is apt to suffer from a neurosis, or in some other way.

These outsiders are in a hopeless position. They have their sexual impulses, like everyone else, but they know that any attempt at gratification will ruin them. They are probably meeting other homosexuals every month of the year, but those they meet cover up their abnormality as anxiously as they do and so they never find any kind of outlet. Even when they are attracted to a man who is an obvious homosexual, they are frightened to make known their desires and dare not be seen in the company of a man whose deviation is too obvious.

It is not unusual for a young man with homosexual tendencies to feel that he is unique. All around him he sees his fellow men taking an interest in girls and yet, to his surprise and shame, he finds that he is aroused by the sight of certain men. This can have the most serious psychological effect. He does not know why he feels as he does; he has never heard of anyone else suffering from a disability so contrary and meaningless, and so he is thrust back into himself, half afraid that he is going insane.

Case XIX. C—— is now 22. He is at present working as a clerk. He has had several jobs and does not seem able to settle down. Here is part of his story:

"I have been interested in other boys since I was about 15 but

137

I cannot remember any sexual desire at that time. My first sexual experience was at 16 when two girls, another boy and myself got very familiar in a field. We all undressed and I became excited through watching the other boy. I went out with girls quite a lot because all my pals did and I used to kiss them and pretend to make love to them. It seemed all rather silly to me, but I went on doing it because it seemed to be expected of me. I was just 17 when I first fell in love with a boy of my own age. I was quite open about it and told him that I loved him and wished he was a girl. He told me to grow up and act like a man. Some time later I had a nervous breakdown. I didn't tell the doctor how I felt about this boy, but I did tell the priest. It was only then that I discovered that there were other people in the world like me. The priest told me that this feeling would soon pass off and I was not to worry about it. When I joined the Army I had a number of sexual experiences with women but it seemed to me to be just like masturbation. I never enjoyed it. I have only had two sexual experiences with men. The first time it was very unexpected; we were both playing around on a sofa and it just seemed to happen. We both felt rather silly about it afterwards. The other time was with a pal in the Army. I had fallen for him, but he didn't seem very interested in me. After I had known him for some weeks, I arranged for him to come home for the week-end. We slept in the same room and I started to undress him as he sat on the bed. When he saw what my idea was, he resisted at first but then gave way and let me carry on. But this is the stupid thing—as soon as I saw that he would let me do what I wanted, I didn't want to have any more to do with him. Of course by this time I had got him excited and so he made me go on with it. Since then I've fallen madly in love three times— all with people about my age. It always works out the same way. I start by admiring them from a distance and wanting to get friendly with them. I'm sure that I don't think about sex to start with, but as I get to know them, the urge to possess them gets stronger and stronger until at last I have to do something about it. When they discover my intentions, they all leave me—one of them hit me, another ran away. Then I'd go home and cry for days and days, and my family would wonder what on earth was the matter with me. I only seem to fall in love with normal people and when I discover that a person is queer, I seem to lose interest. I'd give anything to change. I quite like girls and children. I think I would make a decent husband, but the thought of going to bed with a girl leaves me cold. Each time I fall in love with a man, I really want him as a friend. I don't know why I have to go and spoil it all."

138

Even at the age of 22 this man is sexually immature. He is now being treated by a psychiatrist and there are good chances of a cure. Without this treatment, he would be condemned to a life of misery. His strong guilt complex made it difficult for him to accept other homosexuals. He would try to content himself by admiring others who were heterosexually inclined; but his homosexual tendencies are strong and it proved to be impossible to limit his admiration to a platonic friendship.

All over the country there are thousands of men who are having little or no sexual satisfaction because heterosexuality is as repugnant to them as homosexuality is to the heterosexual. Henry and Galbraith[35] report the case of one patient who vomited whenever he attempted heterosexual relations. Some of them go through agonies of mind trying to fight an abnormality which has been present in them from an early age. Others realize their condition but have neither the means nor the opportunities to practise·their form of sexuality. For the most part, these outsiders are an unhappy lot. A vast amount of suffering is caused, not so much by the lack of opportunities for gratification, but by the simple realization that they are unlikely to make successful husbands or have happy home lives. Many of them feel that the loss of the moral right to found a home is punishment enough without having to take a devious course to satisfy an instinct which most of us enjoy without difficulty.

Although most of the outsiders could never enter any of the other levels of homosexual society for financial, geographical or other reasons, there are a few men who have this opportunity but have remained with the outsiders. Such a man has four alternatives. He can repudiate any kind of sex life; he is unable to enjoy heterosexual relations and he is therefore prepared to repress one of his most powerful natural instincts. It should not be assumed that complete abstinence will necessarily lead to the development of a neurosis. There are some men who, because they are under-sexed, can sublimate these impulses without difficulty. But for most men, some form of sexual activity is necessary for the enjoyment of a full life and mental health.

This homosexual with the free choice may decide to enter at the street-corner level. He has the advantage of remaining anonymous and he can feel that he has no obligations towards his chosen partner. But he will have to mix with (and yet be careful to avoid) the prostitutes, blackmailers and criminals who inhabit these places.

At the "queer bar" level he will find a number of temporary partners and he may experience a measure of short-lived happiness. He will also have to be able to hold his own in a vicious, jealous, back-biting society where no affair is sacred and every effort will be made to hinder his search for happiness.

In the exclusive clubs he is more likely to find someone at his own cultured level and he will meet people who have met and partially solved the same problems that he has had to face. These people are good-mannered, polite and have some respect for the ethics and other moral laws of society, but beneath the façade of contentment he will not find many homosexuals who are inwardly at peace with themselves. The so called well-adjusted homosexual is not without conflict which he may learn to conceal by bravado or express in his contempt for conventionality. The stigma that our society attaches to this abnormality reaches inside the walls of even the most exclusive club.

Few men can choose which level of homosexual society they will frequent, and it can be seen that even those who have this opportunity do not have a very wide or happy choice.

Section VII

THE MIND OF THE HOMOSEXUAL

CHAPTER XXIII

ABSTINENCE OR RECOGNITION

THE CONFLICT WITHIN the mind of the homosexual is created by two directly opposed forces. His powerful sexual impulses drive him in one direction while all the pressures of society force him into other channels. Outwardly the conflict can be resolved, but whichever course he takes, he will still be left with an inner conflict which eats up his energy and saps his vitality. Even the man who decides to abandon the social decrees and lives according to his natural sexual instincts will have more to contend with than the persecution of the community. Inside his mind, the fight has not been won and there will still be the feeling of shame and regret.

This conflict is much more real for the man who is trying to live in conformity with the accepted social rules. If he has faced his problem squarely, he will know that he is sexually aroused by some men and hardly at all by any women. His first reaction will be to ignore these tendencies, to put them out of his mind. But the mind cannot be completely controlled by the will and these impulses will rise again and again. He will succeed in making the impulses seem shameful, but he cannot quite succeed in making the impulses stop working.

Until recently, psychologists were apt to group together all those who were unable to accept the cultural norms and label them as regressive. The homosexual was regarded as immature; he had not grown up sufficiently to understand the obviously realistic and commendable motivations of his own society.

Recent research has shown that very few homosexuals show neurotic symptoms in early life. The mental disorders that many of them acquire are not an original part of their abnormal sexual tendencies but a result of their efforts to suppress these tendencies. Many men in their twenties are thoroughly healthy individuals except for their homosexual tendencies, but after years of having to live their emotional life in secret, or even suppress it altogether,

---

* I am indebted to Dr. Edward Glover for the many suggestions that he made during the preparation of the whole book, and especially for his help with the pathological sections of this chapter.—G. W.

they tend to develop other more serious psychological difficulties. The painful experience of being different from the great mass of people can inflict a psychological wound on an originally healthy person.

The attitude of society can lead to the development of a mental disorder in the homosexual in two ways. Not only is he more likely than the normal man to develop psychopathological reactions on account of the persecution and scorn which he has to endure, but also a neurosis may be precipitated by a mental conflict over his abnormality. While his natural instincts drive him one way and all the pressure of society forces him to act another way, he comes to believe that he is morally unsound and intrinsically worthless.

To understand how this comes about and the varieties of disorder that may ensue, it is necessary at this point to indicate briefly the pathological results of what is now commonly referred to by psychiatrists as *unconscious homosexuality*; this describes individuals with strong homosexual impulses who from childhood onwards have been able to keep these impulses from consciousness only with the help of powerful unconscious defences. So long as these are effective the individual may remain quite unconscious of his tendencies. But when the unconscious defences weaken during adolescence and early adult life, the alternative is either that his impulses should erupt into consciousness, or that he should develop some form of mental disorder.[32]

The gravest of these disorders and certainly the most remarkable of them is that known as persecutory insanity or paranoia. Its beginnings are comparatively simple and can be observed in many individuals.

The individual, weighed down by some abnormal disability (although by this time he does not consciously recognize it), is apt to blame everyone but himself for his failings. The use of the undefined "they" is often heard in this way. "Whatever you do, *they* will always do you down." "They" may refer to the government, the boss, or more often to some vague "evil eye" which sets out to frustrate every attempt at success. This attitude is not unusual in the daily experiences of everyone and in its mildest form it cannot be considered a psychotic condition. But for the paranoid all misfortunes appear to be a personal, continuous and exaggerated attempt to hold him down.

The paranoid type is a difficult, awkward individual who is suspicious, aloof, unfriendly, disgruntled and resentful of authority. Although often clever, and even brilliant, he is never contented. He never feels that the excellence of his work is receiving the credit it deserves so that he frequently changes his job. He will assume that groups of people are talking about him in a disparaging manner. He is always on the look out for slights and sneers and he is quick to detect them where none were intended. He has a continuous persecution complex and in extreme cases he may regress gradually into a chronic delusional state which requires permanent supervision, because he is liable to make sudden and unprovoked attacks upon people who, he supposes, are plotting his downfall.

The contents of the paranoic's delusions often indicate the underlying homosexual thought. Sometimes the individual believes that other men are trying to poison him, or inject noxious substances into him, or disturbing him with electrical waves. He takes the most elaborate precautions against these imaginary tormentors, sets traps, piles the furniture against the door, or refuses food because he is sure that it is poisoned. One case complained that he was always being assaulted with a "syphilis-malaria sponge". This, he said, robbed him of his ribs and back passage. It was his custom to swathe his pelvic regions with masses of newspapers to ward off the attacks by the germs.[4]

Not all homosexuals become even mild paranoids, but nearly all paranoids have repressed homosexual tendencies. Stekel[69] stressed this strong connection when he noted that the content of the hallucinatory and delusional trends in many cases of paranoia and paranoid conditions was frankly homosexual, and the clinical histories in such cases were usually characterized by severe and intractable sexual maladjustments. Freud[29] strongly maintained that "paranoia was dependent upon homosexual fixation and upon repression of homosexuality, partial failure of the repression and consequent projection as symptoms of the repressed homosexual tendencies". Ferenszi[22] went even further and stated that paranoia is nothing else than distorted homosexuality.

Psychiatrists have also found that in cases of chronic alcoholism and drug addiction, the unconscious homosexual factor is often of paramount importance. It has also been recognized that in the common psycho-neuroses, such as the obsessional neurosis or anxiety hysteria, the existence of unconscious homosexuality is an important factor in determining the form of the symptoms. Thus the obsessions of dirt and contamination with their accompanying washing obsessions are often of this nature. Moreover, the internal conflict over the claims of homosexual as against heterosexual impulses is responsible for much of the obsessional neurotic's indecision and doubt and may gradually interfere with his working capacity.[32]

In the case of hysteria two forms of pathological outlet may follow. Either the individual develops one or more of organic disorders affecting different areas or organs of the body, or he falls into anxiety states which take the form of phobias. In the former instance, the location of the disorder is often determined by unconscious homosexual factors (e.g. the stomach and bowel psycho-neuroses). In the latter, the phobias (e.g. of strangers, of social contact with males, of disease) are influenced by the unconscious homosexual factor. Many anxiety depressions are also of this type.

There is yet another form of disorder in which unconscious homosexuality may play a part. This although frequently called an "actual neurosis" is not strictly speaking a "psycho-neurosis" like hysteria. It is due not so much to unconscious conflict as to disturbance in the balance of instinctual energy. The sexual life of the individual with strong unconscious homosexual tendencies rarely run smoothly. It is interfered with sometimes by inhibitions of function, sometimes by excess of function. States of excitation develop which are not given adequate or appropriate discharge, or given excessive discharge.

The results of this vary widely. A state of "anxiety neurosis" may be set up which may take the form of headaches, giddiness, various circulatory and respiratory disturbances, together with apprehensions and general nervousness, until the individual gives up the fight and escapes into what the layman calls "a nervous breakdown". Or the individual may develop a neurasthenia with all the devastating consequences of exhaustion, weakness and instability. Or, again, he may develop what is now called a "psycho-somatic state" affecting body organs in ways that are hard to distinguish from plain hysteria, but are due, not primarily to unconscious conflict, but to pathological excitation. In most psycho-somatic states an unconscious homosexual factor operates, as in the case of diarrhœa or constipation.[32]

These are only a few of the pathological reactions that may follow *unconscious* repression, but they enable us to indicate the lines of mental disorder that may follow the *conscious* conflicts, inhibitions or periodic compensatory excesses of the conscious homosexual who has not come to terms with his problem.

There are many men who believe that they can control their deviation by ignoring sex altogether. They tell themselves that as the only kind of sexual responses that they experience are the wrong ones, they must learn to do without sex altogether. But most psychologists agree that if such an effort of will-power does not result in actual neurosis, it is mentally unhealthy at the very least. Ellis[19] writes: "Experience shows that the majority of people constituting our society are constitutionally unequal to the task of abstinence." Freud says that sexual intercourse acts as a release; it relieves the nervous system of pressure and once the orgasm is over, a compensatory alternative interest is permitted which until then had been blocked by the sexual impulses.[9] Lydston[52] writes: "No man or woman at adult age is in perfect physiological condition unless the sexual function is naturally and regularly performed." Allen[2] writes: "The sexual organs consist of gland and muscle co-ordinated by the nervous system. No other organs are improved by disuse, so why should these be exceptions. Again, the nervous system does not benefit if some instinctual urge is obstructed, and indeed we know for certain that the obstruction leads only to their breaking out in some abnormal channel."

One may argue that the instinctual urge in the homosexual is already abnormal, and this is quite true. But the urge may, if obstructed, be diverted into some more harmful channel.

For example, a few of the cases of men seducing small boys of twelve, eleven, or even younger, are caused by frustrated adult homosexual urges. The adjusted homosexual is no more interested in small boys than the adjusted heterosexual is interested in small girls. There is nothing very surprising in this. The sexual act between two men requires the co-operation of both partners if it is to be successful, just as co-operation between man and woman is necessary for successful coitus. The confirmed homosexual would get no pleasure out of seducing a young boy and would not feel any desire to do so. In fact, most homosexuals do not think young boys are attractive for the very reason that they are too feminine. There is some evidence that the bisexual man finds the effeminacy of extreme youth an attraction to which the homosexual is immune. Infanto-homosexuality, like infanto-heterosexuality, is a separate phenomenon with an ætiology of its own. However it is worth noting that one of the causes may be an obstructed homosexual predisposition; when the control is not complete, the impulse may break out into this anti-social channel.

Other men who are faced with these difficulties argue that sex is only a small part of a man's life; surely it should be possible to concentrate upon the other aspects of life, to keep the mind so occupied that these abnormal tendencies never have a chance to reach the conscious mind. For a time it is possible to surround oneself with so many other activities that it seems as if the sexual impulses are unimportant. But this drive will not lie dormant for a long period and if it is denied expression in the usual sexual outlets, it may tend to find other outlets.

To take first the case of paranoidal regressions or the development of a paranoidal character: it is not, of course, suggested that the abstinence of the conscious homosexual is the fundamental cause of his paranoidal tendencies, but it provides a precipitating factor which in turn is likely to wake up these early tendencies which may not otherwise have disclosed themselves.

As far back as the sixteenth century a man named Weyer[80] first noted the connection between homosexuality and paranoidal hallucinations. He was a quiet, moderate doctor who never made a great name for himself, yet in his recently discovered diaries it was found that he had made a number of original observations which have since become established medical knowledge. At one point he wrote: "I know a sodomite who complained that he always heard passers-by come to cause noise in his ears; even his parents, he said, were doing it; he wrote to me on his own behalf, quite secretly, asking me whether I could give him some advice since some people had told him that his trouble was in his organ of hearing" (from Weyer, *De praestigiis daemonium*, 1579).

The paranoid has rejected homosexuality and has made an effort to achieve the socially accepted goal of heterosexuality with little success. The homosexual drive is twisted around until it turns into persecution. Thus the original "I love him" is unacceptable and becomes transformed into "I hate him". This, too, is unacceptable and so it is projected becoming "he hates and persecutes me". The individual then feels free to hate in return.

The conscious conflict over homosexual behaviour may also lead to the activation of an earlier obsession of hysteria, and so precipitate a classical neurosis. Connor[10] says that "in 90 per cent. of suicidal depressions, the sexual life was unsatisfactory to a marked degree, either in the direction of weakness of the heterosexual urge, or of the strength of the homosexual urge, or both". A great many of the unexplained suicides are the result of the individual's anxiety over his homosexual tendencies. They remain unexplained because the family and friends see little point in bringing this part of the dead man's history to light. There are also a number of suicides after a man has been accused or suspected of homosexual offences.

As for the "actual neuroses" (including anxiety neurosis, neurasthenia and many of the psycho-somatic states), it is obvious that the position of the frustrated or self-frustrated homosexual is excessively prone to set up states of excitation which may lead to these crippling disorders with all their incalculable consequences on personal wellbeing, working and social capacity. This is exacerbated by his reaction to masturbation, which being essentially unsatisfactory to him adds to the general disorder of his instinctual balance.

If the homosexual is to avoid these various psychological

difficulties, he must be able to control or modify his impulses on a realistic basis. He will be unable to do this unless two important factors are present. First, an understanding by the individual of the true nature of his own wayward impulses; and, second, an understanding by the people around him of the source of these impulses. Then the homosexual can acquire an insight into his own motives and, providing the other people in his society have understanding enough not to make the environment conditions too difficult, he can also reconcile these impulses with the outside conditions.

His health of mind depends upon his own self-knowledge and the tolerant understanding of the community. It is, therefore, unfortunate that accurate information is so difficult to obtain because the subject is officially tabooed and the veiled and jesting references to it are misleading.

It should be understood that homosexual tendencies, far from being unusual, are a common factor in the make-up of most men. The realization of their abnormality may fill some men with shame and repugnance but no good can come out of refusing to acknowledge its existence. Homosexuality, like heterosexuality, is a relative condition and varies from one individual to another. If a man is found to have a very strong homosexual tendency, it may be difficult or impossible to re-direct his impulses. But it will still be possible to help him to understand and control these impulses and thereby avoid the far worse consequences of a complicated mental breakdown in later life.

This chapter is not advocating complete sexual freedom for the homosexual or anyone else. It is not suggested that malad-justments and psychological disorders will be cured if all restraints are abolished. But there is little doubt that some emotional difficulties are caused by frustrated homosexual tendencies. The solution is not to be found in uninhibited sexual promiscuity, but in a better understanding of the problem.

CHAPTER XXIV

PERSONALITY

In the previous chapter, it was noted that unconscious repressed homosexuality was often an important factor in the following mental disorders:

(a) Paranoia.
(b) Psycho-neuroses (obsessional and hysterical).
(c) Actual neuroses (anxiety neurosis, neurasthenia, psychosomatic states).

The conscious homosexual who refused to face up to his problem was in danger of frustrating his powerful sexual impulses, and this self-frustration might precipitate a similar mental disturbance. It was also suggested that the homosexual who is prepared to recognize his deviation is more likely to avoid these psychological pitfalls. But the very act of recognizing, modifying and controlling these impulses will have an effect upon his personality.

The ordinary man does not often develop many clear-cut ideas about his reactions to his environment. But the average homosexual has been forced to give more time to thinking about his place in the world; finding that it is sometimes very difficult to conform with the accepted moral code, he has searched for the key to the puzzle. Sometimes this results in the better development of the man's personality, but often the philosophy of the homosexual is neither simple nor satisfactory.

The man who studies the structure of society cannot ignore the desirability of marriage. Even the insurance statistics show that the married man lives longer, enjoys better health, is less likely to succumb to mental illness, is less likely to commit as many crimes, is an all-round better insurance risk. Marriage is also the only approved avenue for satisfying the sexual urges. Many homosexuals earnestly desire marriage and a family life. Their parental instincts are often strong even when they are at variance with their sexual instincts. Sometimes a woman encourages a marriage even when she knows of the man's past homosexual history; she cannot understand, or even believe, that this tendency is anything more than an unfortunate episode that can be cured by the tender care of a loving wife. In addition to the desire for children, marriage can provide companionship, the security of a home, social acceptance, and a sometimes welcome opportunity to leave the parental home.

As a result of this, some people who are quite unfit for marriage undertake it as a kind of social protection. Fortunately most homosexuals avoid this mistake because they are emotionally and romantically untouched by feminine appeal. They are therefore forced to forfeit the advantages of marriage and order their lives in some other way.

A minority of homosexuals swing to the opposite extreme. They pretend to see many disadvantages in marriage, discover homosexuality where it does not exist and pity those who do not suffer from this deviation. Such men will assert that homosexuals are a superior race apart from the common herd, but this arrogance is no more than a defence against their feelings of insecurity and doubt.

The man who openly flouts convention in this way invites social ostracism and he can find satisfactory companionship only among like-minded people. His loneliness and lack of social intercourse will tend to make him look upon sexual intimacy as the only kind of intimacy. But the homosexual who leads a life of self-indulgence pays much the same physical price as the intemperate heterosexual. It is a vicious circle; for his loneliness will drive him into one of the homosexual levels; here he will adopt the vocabulary, mannerisms and customs of this group, and then he will find it even more difficult to gain any kind of social acceptance outside this group.

This may not worry him, for he may be able to attain a measure of happiness within the group. He will learn from the other members how to avoid conflict with the law, although he may get into trouble during one of the sporadic outbursts against "unnatural crimes". Homosexual charges have often been made the exuse for a witch hunt from the dissolution of the monasteries in the sixteenth century to the Rohm purge in Nazi Germany. Should he be arrested in one of the homosexual haunts, he may be convicted of an offence of which he is not technically guilty, on the strength of a suspicious appearance, a strange case-history, or evidence which would be ruled out were he on trial for a more acceptable crime.

But the vast majority of people cannot tolerate a life in which they are punished socially for having a sexual deviation and they consequently conform to the extent of at least giving lip-service.

151

There are some cases of men who have tried to combine an ethical code with overt homosexuality. The sex code may seem to these men to be nonsensical, unreal or untenable; so they have attempted to fit together some sort of ethical code which will line up with their homosexual practices.

Case XX. B—— is a successful business man of 42. He says that he would prefer to have one regular partner but he has not found anyone who shares his own ethical and moral code. He admits that this code is unusual. He does not visit the street-corners, bars or clubs but he has had a number of overt sexual contacts with people he has met "by chance". He will not have sexual relations with another man unless four conditions are fulfilled: (1) He must be an avowed homosexual but not living with or in love with anyone else. (2) He must be over 23. This is an arbitrary age which B—— has selected; his explanation is that they are beyond saving after this. (3) He will only indulge in mutual masturbation. He considers any other form of sexual activity to be perverted. (4) He discourages affection from his partner and if he finds he is getting too fond of a man, he breaks off the relationship. He does not object to paying a prostitute providing these four conditions are fulfilled.

Now this is obviously a home-made ethical code although the individual concerned defends it vigorously, maintaining that no harm is done to anyone and that these occasional sexual outlets enable him to get on with his job without causing trouble. But even when he is quite convinced that he is ethically right, he must carry out these activities in secret and use stealth and deception to obtain his ends. It is doubtful if he is really as satisfied with this arrangement as he makes out. Each time he risks social condemnation and trouble with the police and blackmail. Added to this are other major and minor disadvantages such as loneliness in old age, no real home, no children, no one to care for him when he is sick.

Even if the homosexual has had no overt sexual experience, he must hide his secret, not only from the world at large, but from his closest friends. For most of his acquaintances would be almost as shocked if he confessed to a chaste homosexual love as if he had been found indulging in the lowest sexual vices with other men. This is bound to have some effect upon his general philosophical outlook.

Some writers have attempted to describe the main characteristics of the homosexual's outlook. It has been suggested that he possesses an understanding, a tenderness and a sense of humour not found in the normal man. Others have suggested that he is capable of greater artistic and cultural achievements. But it is unwise to generalize in this way. The deviation will certainly have some effect upon his personality, but the effect will vary according to the basic psychological make-up of the man.

Some will take advantage of the freedom from family responsibilities and devote all their energies and talents to their work or hobbies; others will simply wander, never staying in one place long enough to become a member of a particular community. Some will reduce their social commitments to a minimum and absorb themselves in religious or cultural activities; others will compensate for their lack of family life by cultivating a sociable and convivial disposition.

Although the advantages are outweighed by the disadvantages, it does seem that the homosexual sometimes possesses attributes that can be of value to society as a whole. A contrary sexual impulse is bound to change a man's personality, but the change is not always for the worse.

Section VIII

WHAT CAN BE DONE?

CHAPTER XXV

PREVENTION

I⊤ HAS BEEN FOUND that the possibilities for a cure for homosexuality are strictly limited. When the patient is young or the tendencies are weak, or other favourable conditions are present, many successful cures have been made, but this still leaves a large number of people for whom treatment is useful but a complete cure is unlikely. If this is the only thing that can be done to attack the problem, the outlook would be bleak. In this section it will be suggested that the problem would be less troublesome if three basic changes could be made—a change of heart, a change of law and a change of mind. The first is by far the most important of these because it is a prevention rather than a cure.

There is a homosexual component in all men but the development of these tendencies depends upon the influences surrounding the child in the early formative years. It has been found that seduction has been overemphasized as a cause of homosexuality because in most cases the strength of the tendency has been predetermined in the first ten years or so. It follows that if we are to prevent the development of these tendencies, we must guard against them in the very first years of the child.

In other words, the parents, the guardians, the teachers and other advisers of the young in the past often created the condition in which this disease will flourish. Until we have rid ourselves of false and puritanical attitudes pertaining to sex matters, we are more likely to encourage the spread of this abnormality than to prevent its development.

It is now an established fact that the patterns set in the home will influence the whole of the later life of the child, including the sexual life. Psychosexual disturbances are nearly always found to be the result of difficulties in the child-parent relationship in early childhood. This is particularly likely to cause strong homosexual tendencies to develop when there is some undesirable element in the parent of the opposite sex. Now this refers not only to the mother who neglects and maltreats her boy, but also to the mother who maltreats her son by over-protection—monopolizing, sentimental, over-considerate maltreatment that warps the child's normal development and wrecks his chances of a normal happy life. It is disturbing to think of the number of individuals who could have been happy in a normal life but who have been driven into unhappy homosexuality because of the stupidity, ignorance and pride of their parents.

It is obvious that nagging parents, a drunken or unbalanced father or mother, or almost any lasting unhappiness in the home will have its effect upon the child. The developing child usually finds his most important models in those who stand in parental relationship to him during his early years. Any undesirable qualities in either parent can result in some form of mental sickness, including homosexuality.

It is generally true to say that the child who is sensibly and reasonably brought up, whose questions on sexual matters are adequately answered and whose early sexual activities are treated with polite and friendly understanding, is much less likely to develop sexual abnormalities. When a child develops an interest in its body, his thirst for information must be satisfied unemotionally, calmly—and truthfully. Some parents seem unable to avoid arousing deep anxieties and guilts in the child by threats, warnings and punishments for which he can see not the remotest justification, and which are, in fact, merely a sign that the parents themselves have never satisfactorily overcome their own sexual difficulties. The child should be taught to appreciate that sex is normal, desirable, and not some horrible activity that only exists to be condemned.

Parents and teachers often wonder how old the child should be before he receives his first lessons in sex education. Kinsey found that the age of the first sexual awareness varied so much that it is impossible to select a definite age. For most children the phase of earliest sexual awareness occurs between 8 and 13, but 10 per cent. begin by the time they are 5 years old and other boys of 14 have had no sexual feelings of any kind. The most satisfactory answer to this question is to give the sex information naturally and logically as the questions are asked. In other words, do not set a time apart for a lecture on sex, but let the education follow naturally the child's interests throughout his developing period. This puts most of the work of sex education upon the parents. Unfortunately so many parents have neither the understanding nor the emotional stability to perform the task with success and it is often left to the schoolteachers, who have to deal with the subject in the classroom.

As regards sex education after puberty, it is not often realized that most men reach the peak of sexual activity in their teens. Very few of them are married at this age and any other kind of

158

sexual activity is discouraged. The current social taboos take no account of the strong sexual impulses of the adolescent boy. The result is that these taboos help to drive some men into homosexual practices which they might otherwise have avoided. It would seem that an understanding of the problems and disadvantages of homosexuality would be more valuable to these youths than the usual warning about prostitutes and loose women. Kinsey found that the sexual outlet provided by homosexual relations amounted to three or four times the outlet provided by prostitutes.

Numerous books have been written as a guide to sex education. Most of them keep as far from the subject of homosexuality as possible and mention it only as an adolescent phase which might develop into a repulsive perversion. As over a third of the male population have at some time had homosexual experiences or reactions and 13 per cent. are more homosexual than heterosexual, it would seem that the problem should be considered in greater detail in these books, especially as ignorance is often the cause of the spread of homosexuality.

Parents, teachers, officials and youth advisers are apt to lose all sense of proportion when a boy is discovered to have had homosexual experience. Many misinterpret the meaning of the relationship because they do not realize the incidence and frequency of such activities in the population as a whole. It may well be a passing phase in a boy's history, but if the discovery is exaggerated and misunderstood, it can result in turning the boy away from normal development. In the same way, any attempt to force the boy into masculine pursuits for which he is unsuited can have just the opposite effect and drive him into taking refuge in femininity and passive homosexuality.

The unhealthy influence of the all-male boarding school has already been mentioned. Clifford Allen[2] says: "In the past battles may have been won on the playing fields of our public schools but numerous lives have been broken in the dormitories."

The boy without a sensible and unemotional understanding of sex is most likely to find trouble during his schooldays. His sex education will then come from the other schoolboys and it will be linked to the toilet. It will be a dirty subject, only to be whispered about, giggled about and associated forever with shame and secrecy. He will discover sexual experiences by a trial-and-error process. Parents should also be wary of hero-worshipping attachments to choirmasters, clergymen and youth club leaders, no matter how holy and educational these relationships may seem to be on the surface.

The boy must be encouraged to mix with girls of his own age.

So often the mother's desire to keep her boy for herself "just a little longer" can have an unhappy result. Quite often this mother's jealousy of the boy's girl friends is unconscious. Taking a dislike to each of the girls the boy brings home, putting difficulties in the way of entertaining the girls at home, refusing to recognize that the boy is growing up and developing adult interests—all these little things would be surmounted by the boy with firm heterosexual interests, but they may just be the turning-point in the boy with homosexual tendencies.

Far from discouraging the boy to mix with girls, the parents should worry if he does not show signs of this normal interest in the opposite sex. When such signs are completely absent, the boy should be examined by a trained psychiatrist. Also when the boy is surly, unfriendly, difficult or unsettled, it is often found that he is being troubled by homosexual problems. A psychiatrist can often help the boy to resolve the conflict before it has given rise to a serious mental disturbance.

It has been emphasized that a logical, calm and sensible sex education for the boy can do much to prevent the development of homosexual tendencies. It follows that it is even more important that the parents, teachers, priests, doctors and all who have anything to do with guiding the boy should have a balanced view on sex and should be able to understand the problem of homosexuality.

It is a truism to say that parents do not want their sons to develop into homosexuals. It is fair to assume that they will do almost anything to avoid this misfortune. Yet hundreds of parents are directly responsible for the abnormality of their sons. Many more are indirectly responsible because they form part of the culture that creates and fosters this abnormality.

Now, it is only to be expected that mothers and fathers develop a blind spot where their own boy's emotional future is concerned. They may be aware that homosexuality exists but that such a thing could happen to their own sons is unthinkable. In their eyes the homosexual is a perverted and repulsive criminal, but they disregard the fact that there are hundreds and thousands of them and each one of them was the son of some proud mother and father.

Then, perhaps, the day suddenly comes when it is discovered that the only son, the light of his mother's eyes, is having an illicit affair with another man. Imagine the scene. The mother breaks down in tears of amazement. Perhaps she was wholly ignorant of the existence of this abnormality. It would be hard for her to understand when it happens between two unknown men, but the idea of her own son indulging in such practices is beyond belief. Meanwhile the father will take out whatever is the modern equivalent of the horse-whip. He assumes that the other partner is to blame, for his son comes from a good home, the right class, and there has never been anything like that in his family. There is only one conclusion the father can reach. His son has been seduced; he has become the victim of an evil trick; he knew no better and the other one took advantage of his easy-going nature. The seducer must be made to pay for this; he must be sent to prison; he must be exposed and shamed before the whole community.

Even if the father is right and the son has been seduced, his vengeful attitude is wrong. His son is unlikely to suffer any permanent harm as the result of his homosexual experience providing that it is the first one—and he will not have had many experiences unless he wanted them. A boy can only be seduced once; after the first experience, he cannot plead ignorance. And when the first flush of anger is over, the father may turn to the mother and say: "Why should this happen to us? What have we done to deserve this?" There is a simple answer to both these questions.

A fair understanding of the causes of homosexuality should be part of the education of every parent. Unfortunately the kind of parents who are apt to distort their child's emotional life are just the kind of parents who will be least willing to recognize the damage they can do. Parents must learn to accept the truth that nearly all of us have some degree of homosexual tendencies and sexual abnormality can only be prevented by proper upbringing.

The teacher has an important part to play in the development of a child's emotional life. Many teachers are aware of this responsibility and anxious to do their best but in many cases their own training is woefully inadequate. They are apt to regard any sexual abnormality as a terrible offence and the usual reaction is to expel the child immediately. It is difficult to think of any action that is more likely to convince the boy that he really is abnormal. When the chances of complete cure are so good at this early stage, it is disturbing to think how many boys have been set upon the road to exclusive homosexuality by being held up as shameful examples and driven away from any chance of finding a normal sexual interest.

It is unfortunate that so many men and women enter the teaching profession straight from school, teaching college or university. They will be required to guide a whole host of children and help them out of their adolescent emotional tangles, and yet they themselves have lived all their lives within the security of the academic world and have little knowledge of the problems met in the outside world. In some public schools only unmarried men are allowed to become housemasters, while other men and women are so bedevilled by some abnormality of their own that they are quite unfitted for the task of teaching children.

It is surprising that many doctors still have false and prejudiced ideas about homosexuality. Until fifteen years ago, medical students received no clinical instruction on sexual matters outside the narrow confines of midwifery and gynæcology. This means that the majority of doctors who are practising to-day have had little or no instruction on the sexual abnormalities. Although the medical schools now give a few lectures on the subject, it is certain that more time would be given to it if it was realized how widespread and important the problem is.

The general practitioner who is often the friend of the family rarely hears his patients admit their homosexual tendencies. He may be the friend and confidant of the patient in all sorts of ways outside the realm of medicine, but the sufferer will be careful to hide his homosexuality from someone so well known in his community. Unless the doctor is astute enough to be able to diagnose some mental instability and send him to a psychiatrist, the true source of the patient's trouble will not come to light.

All divinity students should be required to know something about psychology and the problems likely to arise due to sexual difficulties. A minister is often in the position to help homosexuals, for they are apt to regard their problem as a moral issue. They will come to him because they feel that religion is concerned with ultimate and time-tested values. They will be prepared to reveal their thoughts and feelings, and tell the priest those secrets that they have been desperately hiding even from their friends and relations. It is well known that the very act of telling someone one's troubles acts as a useful psychological sedative.

If the minister has taken an interest in the workings of the human mind, he will be able to understand the problem and, if he is unable to help the patient himself, he should be able to pass him on to a competent psychiatrist. On the other hand, the emphasis in the traditional training of some orders makes it difficult for the priest to be helpful. The priest may also regard it as a moral question and he will suggest that will-power and determination are the solutions to the problem. It has already been found that this advice is not just useless; it is dangerous.

Many things can be done to prevent the development of strong homosexual tendencies and most of these concern the proper upbringing of the child because that is when the tendencies

162

originally develop. The infant should, where possible, be treated in a proper biological way from its birth so that fixations are avoided. Elimination training should avoid the implications of nastiness and shame. The child must enjoy the love of his mother, but overprotection and a dominating feminine influence must be avoided. It is important that the boy should be able to mould himself on his father but he should not be forced into masculine pursuits before he is ready for them.

Questions about sex should be answered at any age and sexual information should be given without embarrassment. The growing boy must understand that sex is a natural, normal function and not something to be ashamed of. He should be encouraged to mix freely with children of the same age and of either sex.

So that calm, sensible sex instructions can be given to the child when he requires it, the parents should have some training in, and understanding of, the sexual and psychological development of the child. If homosexual tendencies are discovered or suspected, the boy should be treated by a psychiatrist before further damage can be done to his emotional make-up. Finally, it is clearly the duty of society to provide suitable sex instruction, including an understanding of the sexual abnormalities, for teachers, doctors, clergy, youth club leaders and anyone else who is in a position to influence the emotional development of the boy.

CHAPTER XXVI

MODIFICATION OF THE LAW

THE PROHIBITIONS IMPOSED by the law of this country are based upon the view that sexual conduct is wrong and immoral and cannot be permitted except where it is unavoidable for reproduction purposes. As such it fails to coincide with the customs and culture of any group in our society. As regards the laws that deal specifically with homosexuality, it appears that the idea of the law was to punish heterosexuals who indulged in homosexual practices.

The laws were made and passed many years before the true nature of the homosexual impulse was understood. What we now know is a serious mental disease was considered to be a vice and a crime in those days. The State itself commits a crime when it continues to enrol in the category of vice and crime a phenomenon which is caused by social factors beyond the control of the individual concerned. These laws are left over from the days when people of unsound mind were put in chains or flogged.

The laws were also made and passed long before it was understood that there is a homosexual component in most of us. If the laws relating to homosexuality were rigidly enforced, over one in three of the total male population would have to be segregated from the rest. The high incidence of homosexuality makes these laws unworkable and the result is that a few isolated individuals are punished for an offence which thousands of others commit with impunity. The most tragic consequences of a prosecution are the permanent infamy and social contempt suffered by persons who, without blame to themselves, have a mode of sexual perception diverging from that of the majority.

The laws are also illogical because they apply to men and not to women. Is homosexual intercourse between women less vicious and criminal than homosexual intercourse between men?

Psychiatrists agree that a change of law regarding homosexual offences is long overdue. The medical men are chiefly concerned with the health of the individual, but the lawyer's job is to guard the well-being of society. There is a divergence of opinion among legal men on how to deal with persons charged with these offences.

Some members of the legal profession still nourish the primitive and mostly superstitious belief in the virtue of punishment. Kenny[44] says the purposes of punishment are deterrent, both to the offender and to others, and reformative; the subsidiary purposes are the gratification of the person injured and the satisfaction of the indignation of the community.

The threat of prison may act as a deterrent to some homosexuals. At any rate it will create a condition of anxiety bordering on the neurosis and force them into seeking their emotional satisfactions by secret and underground methods. But the sexual drives are very strong impulses and just as the heterosexual will sometimes risk his career, his security and even his life to obtain his ends, so the homosexual is motivated by equally powerful impulses. The figures for reconvictions among homosexual offenders is not noticeably higher than for reconviction for other offences, but it is doubtful if this is the result of the deterrent effect of prison. It is more likely that the ostracism of society that every homosexual offender meets when he comes out of prison has forced him to give up any attempt to abide by the normal social conventions and he has joined the ranks of the experienced homosexuals. These are the sort who do not often get into trouble with the law as they have learnt to find their way around at one of the levels of homosexual society.

This does not apply to the infanto-homosexuals, who can find no level where their practices are approved and they come up before the courts again and again. Each time the prison sentences get longer, but the infanto-homosexual shows no sign of being cured of his perversion. When a doctor gives a patient a medicine, if he does not improve, he may double the dose; but if he still does not improve, the doctor will look for another remedy. The law continues to double the dose of imprisonment on the infanto-homosexual. Not only is this stupid, but it is against the interests of society to condemn the offender to prison repeatedly and then allow him to come out and mix freely with the population, knowing full well that he is even more likely to commit the very same acts. It is more like a council of despair than a rational method. The deterrent effect of prison is very small, and the reformative effect is non-existent. Prison does not reform homosexuals; it breeds them.

As regards the subsidiary purposes of punishment as suggested by Kenny, the gratification of the person injured does not apply except in the cases of child victims of infanto-homosexuals. It is agreed that they are entitled to some measure of gratification although the moral and mental injury done to the child has been overemphasized by officials of the law. There is little doubt that the last subsidiary purpose of punishment—the satisfaction of the indignation of the community—is often amply fulfilled by the harsh penalties meted out for homosexual offences. But a principle involving the satisfaction of social indignation is not, in itself, above suspicion.

An argument against changing the law is that magistrates and judges are slowly getting more tolerant of homosexual offences and the Criminal Justice Act and other reforms are bringing about a more enlightened attitude. It is true that the interpretation of the law is not so prejudiced as it was. The fate of the homosexual offender now depends upon the wisdom and discretion of the magistrate. Some of them have an intelligent understanding of the nature of the disease; others are not swayed by medical opinion even when it is available and their own interpretation of the law is their only guide.

Even when psychological treatment is provided in prison, it is doubtful whether the best efforts of the psychotherapist will not be nullified by the influences of that environment. Often the effects of the treatment are lost when the offender has to meet the displeasure of the outside world. One of the essential parts of a course of psychological treatment is the training the patient receives in fitting himself into the ordinary life of the community. The psychiatrist who is working within the confines of a prison wall not only has to work on the patient's original difficulties, but also has to combat the pressures of this unnatural environment. Nor can the psychiatrist see if this approach is proving effective until the patient has been brought into contact with ordinary conditions.

The overriding consideration in dealing with homosexual offenders should be that it is a form of mental sickness. A revision of the law on the lines of the *Code Napoléon*, accepted by most civilized countries a century ago, would still provide for the protection of children and public decency. It should not be difficult to draw a sharp line between the infanto-homosexual and a relationship between two men who fully understand what they are doing. Psychiatrists agree that although the two impulses may stem from the same roots, "there is a sharp differentiation between those homosexuals who have boys as an object and those who are attracted by men; it is not at all common to find a man greatly attracted by both".[16]

The persistent seducer of young boys must be segregated, permanently if necessary, but the first offender should be regarded as a psychiatric case and remanded for appropriate treatment. Nor should it be assumed in these cases that the seducer is automatically a fiend and the child is blameless. Children sometimes go to great lengths to tempt a man into committing an offence with them. It should also be remembered that children's evidence, especially as regards to sexual matters, is notoriously unreliable; this point has often been stressed by many medico-legal authorities.[1]

Edward Glover of the Institute for the Scientific Treatment of Delinquency[31] has suggested one way of dealing with these cases. He points out that under the Juvenile Delinquency Acts, the law covered new ground by setting up two categories for children "in need of care and protection" and children and adolescents "out of control". Among the cases "in need of care and protection" come a number of children who because of bad family conditions are thought to need not only care and protection but to require preventative supervision.

He points out that by establishing the category "in need of care and protection", society has admitted its responsibilities for one particular group. He now suggests that there is no good reason why this "protecting" principle should not be applied to groups suffering from some sexual abnormality.

The infanto-homosexual will then be charged with an offence against public decency. If it is a first offence, he will not be fined or imprisoned but bound over on set terms of treatment and supervision. He might be allowed to live at home with probationary control, continue with his work unless the psychiatrist advises against it, and undergo a course of psychological treatment. Where the treatment is intensive, the probationary supervision could be waived. If the offender fails to continue with the treatment or fulfil the set conditions of probation, the power of the Court can be amply maintained by a Contempt of Court system. Failure to comply with the conditions set by the Court would constitute a Contempt of Court and the offender could be punished according to the seriousness of the offence. If the offender commits another offence while still under treatment, this also could be considered as a Contempt of Court although it would not be sensible to inflict penalties on the offender until it was certain that all efforts at treatment had failed.

Obviously this procedure should apply only to first offenders. Some cases of infanto-homosexuality have been neglected for so long that there is little hope that any kind of treatment will be of much value. For example, there is the case of the scoutmaster who will be 60 by the time he has completed his latest sentence of fourteen years and who will have spent twenty-three of his sixty years in prison all for the same offence.[66] There will be a number of similar cases where segregation is essential for the protection of the community. But the offender should not be sent to prison for a predetermined number of years and then released irrespective of the fact that he is in the same or worse condition as when he committed the offence.

The Court should give the man an indeterminate sentence and he should not be allowed to inflict his abnormality upon the community until it is reasonably certain that he can control it. If this means that some cases will be segregated for the remainder of their lives, even this solution is better than sending a man to prison three or four times without doing anything to cure his disability. Indeed, there is good reason to believe that there will not be many habitual and incorrigible offenders if the infanto-homosexual was given appropriate treatment after the first offence.

Where temporary segregation is necessary, the offender should be sent to some special clinic. Under existing conditions this would involve residence at an in-patient psychiatric centre, but not, of course, in any department where border-line or certified insane cases are admitted. But it would be far more satisfactory if there were some special clinics for psychosexual conditions to which the courts could send these cases for psychotherapy.

Such a clinic would have many advantages. It would provide material for intensive research into infanto-homosexuality and into other psychosexual disorders, and from this it is hoped that better solutions of these problems will emerge. The psychiatrists in these special clinics would be working on this one type of case and would be certain to become more skilled than otherwise. This would result in greater advances being made and more patients would be cured. It should not be impossible to run the clinic in such a way that the inmates could still be made to contribute to the welfare of the community and it is well known that many infanto-homosexuals have much to contribute. The discharge of the offender from the clinic would not depend upon the gravity of his offence or the time that he had spent there, but upon his ability to control his abnormality and conform with the existing social and legal code.

In the not far distant future it may be possible to allow infanto-homosexuals who are beyond the scope of psychiatric treatment to regain their liberty if they agree to submit to castration or œstrone treatment. Voluntary castration is already used in Denmark for the treatment of sexual offences. Dr. Sturup[71] reports that the castrated "refer to the sense of peace and confidence in their behaviour which follows the operation". But there are many reports of continued sexual activity in men who have been castrated. The effect seems to vary from individual to individual; even the Romans noted that some eunuchs were not safe to be left alone with the women slaves. It is believed that further research will have to be made into the effects of castration and œstrone treatment (reported in Chapter IX) before these methods can be applied.

As regards homosexual relations between two men, there are some unhappy examples of legal enforcement where the offence has occurred between two consenting adults who in other respects are perfectly law-abiding, social, and respectable citizens. One such case resulted in six years' prison sentence. It is far from clear that overt homosexuality between adults is a matter for the law to interfere with.

When the law is enforced in these cases it cannot claim to be protecting anyone, for no one is disturbed in any way by intercourse between two men who fully understand what they are doing. It is a mistake to think that the law should have any hand in enforcing moral, ethical or religious principles. Time and again it has been proved that people cannot be persuaded to "do good by statute". But if the law is amended so that homosexuality between two consenting adults is no longer an offence, there will have to be important exceptions. Children and youths will have to be protected; any kind of violence must still be illegal; public decency must be maintained; and soliciting and prostitution must be controlled.

Children can best be protected by establishing an age of consent for boys as well as girls. Offenders who indulge in homosexual activities with boys below this age should be treated as suggested on pages 167 and 168. When both partners are above this age, such activities should not constitute a legal offence. As the sexual development in boys is subject to wide variation, it is difficult to determine exactly what age should be the age of consent. At all events it is a decision that should be made by a committee of experienced psychiatrists rather than left in the hands of the lawyers.

Just as in heterosexual relations, any activity in which one of the partners is an unwilling participant should be made illegal. Most of the outbursts of violence are usually the sign of psychological weakness rather than strength, but the public must be protected from any activities that result in injury or harm. The present law on assaults could probably be applied to such cases. It would be much to the advantage of the community if the law would stop worrying so much about the control of individuals with homosexual tendencies, and would concern itself with the control of men, both heterosexual and homosexual, who use aggression, fraud, trickery or violence to force other people into sexual relations.

169

The performance of homosexual activities in public places and offences against the public decency can be dealt with by the Common Law of the country, and no further legislation is necessary. Homosexual activities carried out in private offend no one and should be beyond the arm of the law. Society is entitled to protect itself against acts of public indecency but it is not entitled to "punish" psychological disorders.

Soliciting for immoral purposes and the procuring of male prostitutes can be dealt with under the same laws as those which apply to female prostitutes. No one can pretend that this is a very satisfactory arrangement and it is hoped that some more enlightened solution to the whole problem of prostitution will become available in the not too distant future.

Therefore it is suggested that Sections 61 and 62 of the Offences Against the Person Act of 1861 should be repealed and the words "in private" should be deleted from Section 11 of the Criminal Amendment Act of 1885. An exception should be made by establishing an age of consent for boys and the other exceptions can be dealt with under the existing law.

The strongest argument against making it legal for two men to have homosexual relations together is that bi-sexuals and men with only weak homosexual tendencies will be tempted to indulge where they would otherwise have abstained. This is a fair argument and it may well be true in some cases. But if a man with weak tendencies does at one period of his life indulge in homosexual relation and then returns to normal sexuality without being dragged through the mud of the magistrates' court and enmeshed in all the paraphernalia of criminal litigation, he will be much better off than the man who is sent to prison and returns to society spiritually and morally broken. It cannot be denied that this suggested change of law may result in some people having homosexual relations who might otherwise have avoided them—until later in life at any rate. But it is unlikely that this change will greatly increase the incidence of homosexuality. It must be remembered that it is not the regular practising homosexuals who get caught. The law is most effective in catching those who try to abide by the law.

No solution to this problem can be perfect until we have learnt how to prevent the development of these tendencies. But the added temptation to the abstinent homosexual is offset by some very real advantages. The most important of these is that the temptation towards infanto-homosexuality will be considerably reduced. Time and again it has been found that the man who has attempted to repress his homosexual tendencies has only succeeded in diverting them towards young children. Practically all the cases where a cultivated and socially-minded man has had a lapse in later life concern the seduction of young children. Surely it is better that two like-minded men should indulge together than that one man should give way to a sudden impulse and seduce one of our children.

Other advantages of a change of the law are that the activities of the blackmailer will be curtailed; here is a factor which concerns both heterosexuals as well as homosexuals. Also, the anti-social influences in practising homosexuals and the development of paranoid conditions or other neuroses in abstaining homosexuals will both be considerably reduced. Finally, a number of people will be able to go through a homosexual period and then will be able to reject it and adjust themselves to heterosexual intercourse without having to face the penalties of the law which would almost certainly have turned them into exclusive homosexuals.

The advantages of a change of law outweigh the disadvantages. This is not really surprising when it is remembered that the existing law is ineffective and unworkable. For hundreds of years the law has been trying to control homosexuality by vicious persecution and an unfounded belief in the deterrent value of imprisonment. Its best efforts have failed. The time has come to try another method.

CHAPTER XXVII

TOLERANCE AND UNDERSTANDING

I<small>T WOULD BE A</small> mistake to put too much blame on the officials of the law for their intolerant attitude towards homosexuality. A magistrate has to contend with the heavy pressure of public opinion and many of them who have tried to apply the recent discoveries of psychological medicine while judging a case have been called "soft". They are in a particularly difficult position when dealing with an abnormality that engenders strong emotions and blind prejudices. When one magistrate decided to remand a homosexual offender for treatment, a policeman was heard to say that the offender escaped a prison sentence because the magistrate was "an old queer himself". Of course this is nothing more than ignorant and vituperative abuse, but magistrates are only human, and must live and work in the community like everyone else; they cannot be blamed too much if they tend to utilize the findings of psychiatry only to the extent that the community will back them. Until the whole of society is prepared to regard homosexuality as a mental disorder, we cannot expect much change in the attitude of magistrates and judges.

So far the attitude of most sections of society has, if anything, been more uncompromising than the attitude of the lawyers. This is almost entirely due to ignorance—an ignorance that has little chance of being alleviated because the whole subject is surrounded with secrecy and suspicion. All such activities are considered to be perverse and unnatural, although the latter is an epithet the validity of which will not survive even the most cursory study of Nature.

Almost all men have a homosexual component in their make-up and this, twisted into a subconscious fear, is often the cause of the uncompromising attitude towards homosexuality. The general public should recognize that these tendencies are present in almost every man and almost anyone could be converted into a homosexual if unfavourable circumstances were present during childhood, or in an unusual situation, such as a prisoner of war camp.

172

It is imperative that the subject be discussed openly and without embarrassment. The secrecy and shame that surrounds the subject at present gives it the aura of forbidden fruit which is unwise and unhealthy. As a topic of conversation sex is not really very interesting because it is mainly sensory and does not lend itself well to words. The only thing that keeps alive the everlasting dirty stories and the mines of sexual misinformation is that it is a forbidden topic, to be whispered and giggled at in dark corners. If the subject were brought out into the clear light of day, it would hold little interest as a subject of conversation. In this chapter it will be suggested that the present attitude of society to homosexuality is wrong and should change. It is never possible to plan or produce a sudden alteration in public opinion, but it is believed that if the problem were better understood, most thinking people would agree that the present attitude is unfair and unreasonable.

As a nation we are renowned for our tolerance and our ability to recognize individual differences. Up and down the country, one can find a bewildering array of beliefs, crusades and modes of living. In the main, the British man is ready to smile tolerantly at whatever his neighbour is up to and he expects, and gets, the same recognition for his own individual differences. It is only when he fails to understand the underlying motives that he displays signs of intolerance.

Until recently we were not prepared to extend this tolerant attitude to anything connected with sex, but nowadays the views and actions of the average man are far more liberal than the legal and social rules of the sex code. Indeed the tolerance allowed to the promiscuous male is quite surprising when one considers that our whole social system is based upon the family unit. In some sections of our community a man's reputation is enhanced by the number of women he has had; if he has managed to seduce a woman who is normally regarded as inaccessible, he will brag about the conquest to his fellow men and far from being disgusted by him, they will be proud to have such an expert seducer as a friend.

This attitude of admiration for the promiscuous male is not, of course, shared by all, but there are signs that it is spreading. Many will think that such freedom is going too far and it certainly is not suggested that the community's attitude to homosexuality should be like this in any way. But it is an example of the fact that our attitude to sex is changing and it raises the hope that, at some future date, people will be able to understand the problem of sexual abnormality. Then they will prefer to seek a remedy rather than persecute and ridicule the sufferers. Considered

173

calmly without emotion or prejudice, the homosexual act is probably less dangerous to society than sexual promiscuity, adultery or prostitution.

There are many good reasons why society should alter its attitude to the homosexuals. The cause of the abnormality comes from within society. The effect of persecution sometimes drives a man into explicit homosexuality. The cure of the disease is made much more difficult because a man will try to hide his tendencies and dare not seek advice about them.

When it is understood that the homosexual is involved in behaviour that is not fundamentally different from that followed by over a third of the male population at some period of their lives, society must consider these activities in an altogether different light. Before people start to condemn homosexuality, they should remember that "forty per cent. of all males could be arrested at some time in their lives for similar activity and twenty to thirty per cent. of the unmarried males could have been arrested for homosexual activities that had taken place within that same year".[45] The incidence is such that, whatever the moral rights and wrongs of the problem, it is not physically feasible to stamp it out.

Most parents refuse to believe that homosexuality is a problem that could cause any difficulties for their own sons. When they are aware of the problem, their knowledge is so faulty that, far from adopting the right kind of upbringing to prevent the development of this tendency, they are apt to drive their sons to seek shelter in femininity by forcing them to adopt masculine pursuits to which they may be quite unsuited. It would be much more sensible if society would take a boy as he is and fit a moral code to him, instead of twisting him to comply with a pre-determined sex code.

Another good reason why we should stop driving the homosexual into underground activities is that we cannot afford to lose the talents and gifts of so large a proportion of the nation. Many homosexuals have much to contribute to the welfare of the community. Are we prepared to forgo all their skills and abilities in order that we can satisfy some cruel and outdated moral law?

It must be said in all fairness that there are a few people in this country who have faced the problem and realized that the present attitude of society is not in accord with the practices of a civilized country. But they cannot bring themselves to agree with an alteration of the law and a social toleration of homosexuality because it is a biological blind alley. They argue that any sexual relationship between two men is completely un-

174

biological and as such is a menace to the prosperity of the community.

The scales are heavily weighed in an argument like this when years of faulty teaching has made it difficult to regard sex as anything but a means of reproduction. The biological argument against homosexuality is uncontestable for those who see sex as a mere bodily function, a mechanical relief unadorned by either love or mutual sharing.

The crude animalism of this attitude is not even found among the lower vertebrates. Professor Hooton[20] compared the sexual behaviour of the anthropoid apes with that of human beings: "It must not be imagined that our ape peers or monkey inferiors remain virtuously continent except at definite and restricted breeding seasons. On the contrary, sexual activity—both heterosexual and homosexual—occurs almost unintermittently, but it is often of a social and symbolic character rather than strictly utilitarian. Sexual behaviour without reproductive consequences seems to be a perfectly natural primate amusement and it is sheer nonsense to pretend that some natural or divine law restricts lower or higher animals to mating for revenue only."

The proposition that sex is solely a device for the propagation of the race is an idea that we have inherited from the old Jewish sex code. As they were a small tribe hemmed in on all sides by large hostile tribes, they may have had good social reasons for adopting such an attitude. The Christian theologians seem unable to shake off this idea which was no more than a practical solution to a pressing problem of the times; theological arguments that true love is consummated only through children and that only thus is it pleasing in the sight of God, take no account of the economic and social problems of to-day, nor of the discoveries of modern psychological medicine.

If the nation was in danger of dying out, this argument would be easier to understand. If it is true that our first consideration must be an increase of the birth-rate, then other methods would be much more effective. All bachelors, celibate priests and unmarried women should logically be under society's disapproval. Contraception of any kind should be considered a crime. We should adopt Hitler's ideas and reward illegitimacy with specially sunny nursing homes—the child to remain in the care of the State, the mother to return home to carry on with the good work.

In fact, there are no grounds for supposing that a change of attitude to homosexuality will decrease the birth-rate. Here is part of an anthropological report by Harrison[33] on the big Nambas, a tribe which lives in Malekula in the New Hebrides: "The first thing one notices among the big Nambas is the way the

175

men go around behind the boys and the boys are the fond servants to the men. This homosexuality system is ancient, with its own technique and nomenclature, relationship regulations as to which boys you may like. Each man has his boy if he can get one; he guards him more jealously than his female wife. The two often grow very fond of each other. Men who have boys have one or more wives and children. There are more children per head in this area than in any part of Malekula. The women have a parallel pleasure system."

Nor are there any indications that the birth-rate is affected in the European countries that do not outlaw homosexuality. In Turkey, where homosexual practices are recognized and approved social behaviour, the population has continued to rise.

The politicians and economists worry about the rising or falling birth-rate, but the ordinary man is quite right to think more about the health and happiness of single children. The homosexual who is forced into an unsatisfactory marriage by the attitude of society is more likely to bring into the world a child whose upbringing in an unhappy home will not result in an ideal addition to the population of the nation.

Another strong argument against a more tolerant attitude has been put this way: It is all very well saying that homosexuality is a disease, but what if your own son was seduced? What would be your attitude then?

First it is important to note that if the son was still young when he was seduced, it would be the work of an infanto-homosexual. It is no part of the plan to advocate that licence should be given to men who seduce small boys. It is advocated that society should be much more tolerant to homosexual relationships between two adult men, but society must at all times reserve the right to protect its children against these seductions of the infanto-homosexual.

When a young boy is seduced by an elderly boy or an infanto-homosexual, the parents will immediately assume that the seducer is entirely to blame. This assumption may not be correct, but it is only natural for them to blame someone else. The easiest way out of the problem would be to report the matter to the police and let them take action to see that the older boy or man does not seduce any more children until he returns from prison. But this would not be the most satisfactory solution to the problem.

The father's first duty is to his son, and the social aspect, the protection of other children, is a secondary but important factor. If the son has had a good upbringing and has not developed strong homosexual tendencies, the effects of the seduction will be small. It has happened and is happening to thousands of young boys every year and most of them get over it and develop normal sexual outlets. If this is not the boy's first homosexual experience or if the parent has any reason at all to suspect that these homosexual tendencies are more than a passing phase, he should send the boy to a psychiatrist for treatment. At this early age, there is every hope that the boy can be successfully treated. If the psychiatrist reports that a complete cure is not possible, the parent should remember that the damage was not done at the time of seduction, but many years before, and that he is, in part, responsible for the condition of his son.

This attitude is expecting rather too much of the average parent as things are to-day, but if he were an enlightened man he would also realize that it is useless to send the older boy or man to prison. He should persuade the seducer to go and see a psychiatrist. The parent is unlikely to need threats or coercion to persuade him, because most infanto-homosexuals are acutely aware of the hopelessness of their condition and are anxious to do something, almost anything, about it. If the man is depraved and it is obvious that he does not want to be cured, then he must be segregated from the community and sent to some special clinic where he will remain until his condition is improved.

This would be the sensible, logical and best action for a parent to take. But it is a counsel of perfection. All the pressures of society, the attitudes of the parent's neighbours and friends would demand retribution. Just as the attitude of society was, directly or indirectly, a factor in the original seduction, so the current attitude of society will be the cause of disgracing and shaming the boy with sordid interrogations and half-hidden implications that he is already a lost soul, while the older boy or infanto-homosexual will be sent to prison where his condition will be aggravated, until he is let out to repeat the performance all over again.

It has been argued that the time when homosexuality is permitted and tolerated coincides with the period when the nation as a whole starts to decline and degenerate. This argument is not borne out by historical evidence and is the result of illogical thinking. Some people argue a priori on the basis of certain subjective ethical and moral concepts that, because such activities are deemed to be morally wrong, therefore they cannot fail to produce disastrous effects upon the whole nation. For many years children were told that they would go insane if they gave way to the desire to masturbate. Venereal disease was considered to be the just reward for illicit relations. There never has been any logic or sense behind such statements, but they were accepted as the truth because they dealt with subjects where morality overruled the claims of logic and sense. Clear thinking is equally rare when the subject of homosexuality is discussed.

In the last three chapters, it has been suggested that changes can be made in the way we bring up our children, in the law as regards homosexuality and in the social attitude that we adopt towards homosexuals. It is believed that no serious objection will be made to the first suggestion. It is chiefly a matter of counteracting ignorance in order to prevent the development of homosexual tendencies. The second and third suggestions will not be accepted without serious opposition. No miracles are expected and any change will have to come gradually after further discussions and much thought.

One of the results of such discussions will be to bring the question out into the open. This alone will be repugnant to many people. It will seem to them that the incidence of homosexuality will increase when it is no longer shrouded in secrecy. Homosexuals who have for years practised in secret will be less afraid to discuss their difficulties, and at first it may well give the impression that the disease is on the increase. A psychiatrist[54] is reported to have said:

"The story of sexual difficulties is similar to, let's say, appendicitis. Years back a lot of people died from peritonitis following a ruptured appendix, but their deaths were diagnosed as being caused by anything from stomach complaint to heart failure. Then a number of doctors and surgeons began to perfect techniques of diagnosis and surgery for appendicitis, but the cause was given as appendicitis, thanks to these new techniques and to the dissemination of information among medical men. Casually looking over the mortality figures for a period of twenty years in the early part of the century, one could conclude that appendicitis was on the upswing—actually the opposite was true. People who would have died from appendicitis were being saved, and those who couldn't be saved were listed under the correct cause of death."

In the same way it may appear at first that the incidence of homosexuality is on the increase because more will be known about it and more men will apply for treatment. But again, the opposite will be true. People will be more aware of the problem, parents will take preventative measures, men with homosexual tendencies will not hide them away but take steps to deal with them, and the overall number of homosexual men will decrease.

The proselytizing effects of homosexuality are much misunderstood. Certainly there are some influences that tend to

178

stamp in a certain pattern of behaviour. But they are no more powerful in sexual matters than in anything else that involves pleasure or pain. Broadly speaking, a behaviour pattern is formed under three principles. (1) An activity that brings about a pleasurable emotion will be repeated, or at least, the individual will attempt, consciously or unconsciously, to repeat that activity. (2) An activity which invokes considerable pleasure will tend to exclude other activities which might otherwise have been found satisfying. (3) The pleasure enjoyed from a particular activity can be passed on to other activities which were closely associated with it when the original pattern was being formed. The same three principles apply in reverse: An individual will attempt to avoid an activity that once gave pain; a pet hate can exclude other dislikes; an association with an unpleasant event can bring on displeasure.

The first overt homosexual experience can then have varying effects. For the man with strong heterosexual tendencies, the experience will be unsatisfactory, even repulsive. This will tend to strengthen his heterosexual tendencies and increase his dislike of homosexual associations. For the man with strong homosexual tendencies, the first overt experience will tend to strengthen these tendencies. But as we have found that the man with strong tendencies is almost sure to find an outlet sooner or later, the effect is not very large.

In other men the sexual balance is so delicate that the first sexual experience is important. If, due to lack of adequate sex education, the first heterosexual experience is unpleasant, painful or unsuccessful, there may be a great reluctance to repeat it. He may decide, after such an unhappy experience that he really is homosexual and he may give up all attempts to adjust himself to heterosexuality. If his first experience is homosexual and he already has a predisposition in that direction, he will tend to continue with that kind of behaviour. He will assume that he is homosexual because he obtains pleasure from these activities, whereas if the subject were not taboo and if he were aware that many men have indulged in similar activities but developed normal heterosexual reactions later, then he would not so readily abandon himself to this abnormality. In other words, men with slight homosexual tendencies are turned into overt homosexuals not so much by an early experience, but by ignorance of the meaning of that experience and an inability to see it in its true perspective.

Nor is the frequency of intercourse between established homosexuals likely to increase even when the law and society ceases to condemn these practices. The strength of the sexual drive varies in homosexuals just as it does in heterosexuals. Some require many contacts a week, others are content with only very occasional experiences. When sex is easily obtained, most people find that it is no burden to control their desires and over indulgence is no temptation. Even Homer's Greeks knew this. For when Aphrodite outbid Pallas and Hera for the Golden Apple which Paris held, she offered—and he accepted as the best bid—not the fairest wife in Greece, but "inexhaustible lust".

CHAPTER XXVIII

CONCLUSIONS AND FIRST OBJECTIVES

THE ARAPASH, A PEACEFUL and well-organized tribe in New Guinea, often sit in the mud as they work or relax, but they never go to the seaside and sit on the sands, which they regard as filthy. It is a small point, but it would be very difficult to persuade them that the people who sit in the sun at Brighton are right, and they are wrong.

Many of the attitudes and modes of living in our civilization are accepted without question. This is especially true of the things that are not openly discussed. The spread of knowledge is particularly slow when the information infringes on one of our social taboos. It is no wonder that the problem of homosexuality is clouded with ignorance and hidden by prejudice.

It is believed that this problem is much greater than most people realize and enters and disturbs many seemingly unrelated parts of our social organization. It is also believed that no progress can be made towards solving this problem until the subject is allowed to come out into the open.

Whether or not any progress can be made towards solving the social problem of homosexuality depends in the last analysis upon an invisible but potent force—public opinion. If the facts were better known, the normal individual, to whom codes of decency are neither a temptation nor a burden, would realize how much he has in common with those who suffer from a contrary sexual impulse.

The disease is the outcome of constitutional factors aggravated by environmental and social disharmonies. It is produced *in* society *by* society. When the problem is recognized and openly discussed, the public will realize that here is a sexual activity that has always been a part of the pattern of the human mind. While the statistical prevalence of a practice is no guide to its desirability, it should act as an indication that the problem cannot be solved by ignoring it.

The roots of our present attitude seem to be firmly embedded in the belief that the code of conduct which exists at the present moment is right beyond question, and therefore any research into

181

the problem is, in itself, morally wrong. None of the victories dealing with enlightened sex ethics have been won without a struggle. This is not expected to be an exception.

Many years ago Ivan Bloch[7] suggested that "enlightenment would be helpful if those homosexuals who belonged to the better classes would freely and openly admit their tendencies". This is not a very practical suggestion, but there is little doubt that, if it were followed, there would be many surprises. This is a problem that reaches from the lowest to the highest in the land. Instead of persecuting and ridiculing an individual about his emotional handicap, it is suggested that society would do better to show more concern over his mental qualities and social capabilities than over anything in his sexual history.

From the standpoint of biology, homosexuality is a senseless and aimless phenomenon, but it is not the only one in nature—the human cæcum, for example, is a part of the intestine which appears to be quite useless. From the standpoint of humanity, there are several hundred thousand in this country alone who owing to causes quite beyond their control are deprived by society of the reasonable satisfaction of instincts which are the foundation of human happiness. In the light of all the facts presented in this book, it is believed that the time has come to re-form our social attitude towards the homosexual, to abandon ignorant prejudices and ancient restrictions irrelevant to the conditions existing to-day.

The chapters in this book have been grouped into eight sections. From each of these it is possible to draw broad general conclusions.

I. The problem of homosexuality is largely ignored by the general public. When the subject is unavoidable, ignorance and invective make it almost impossible to discuss the subject without emotion. The incidence of homosexuality is far greater than has been recognized hitherto. Nearly all men have a homosexual component in their emotional make-up. There is no sharp dividing line between a homosexual and a heterosexual. Instead there is a kind of sexual balance and a man may be at any point between the two extremes of heterosexuality and homosexuality.

II. The chief cause of the development of homosexual tendencies is maladjustment during early childhood. A man who develops only weak tendencies may pass through a homosexual phase and then adjust himself to normal sexual outlets without difficulty. A man with strong homosexual tendencies is almost sure to experience overt sexual relations at some period of his life. Seduction can be the turning-point in the sexual history of a man, but its influence has been overemphasized. Most men will

182

succumb to homosexual practices if the circumstances are sufficiently unusual—such as an all-male environment.

III. The only antidote known at present is lengthy psychiatric treatment. The chances of complete cure depend upon the strength of the tendency and are strictly limited, but most homosexuals benefit from a course of psychotherapy. As the tendencies are developed in early childhood, they are for the most part beyond the conscious control of the individual and so will-power and self-suggestion are of little help in bringing about a cure, and by themselves are worse than useless.

IV. Throughout history the law in this country has attempted to stamp out homosexuality by vicious persecution. Even the death penalty failed to put a stop to these activities, while the effect of prison sentences was found to aggravate the disease rather than cure it. All the laws dealing with this offence were made over seventy years ago, long before the discovery of modern psychological medicine.

V. The attitude of other communities towards homosexuality has varied throughout history, but the British attitude has always been one of ridicule and disgust. These activities are still considered to be a deliberate perversion, and anyone who is found to have had homosexual experience is ostracized by the community. The reasons for this attitude are: (1) Ignorance of the real causes of its development and a failure to recognize that it is a disorder of the mind. (2) A guilt complex caused by the projection of the suppressed homosexual component that exists in most men.

VI. The man who attempts to adjust himself to his abnormality must enter one of the levels of homosexual society. Since the homosexual finds that an important part of the moral code is unworkable as far as he is concerned, he tends to question and reject other parts of the moral and ethical codes. Consequently most levels of homosexual society are sordid, if not frankly antisocial. But the majority of men with homosexual tendencies do not adjust themselves to their abnormality and often attempt to conform with the existing moral code by abstaining from all sexual outlets. The results are often tragic because the sexual drives will not lie dormant for ever, and after years of control a sudden outbreak can lead to disgrace and imprisonment.

VII. Sexual abstinence does not provide a solution for most homosexuals. Many of those who suppress these powerful impulses are liable to develop some kind of psychological difficulty. The pathological reactions that follow unconscious repression indicate the lines of the mental disorder that may follow conscious frustration. An understanding of the true nature of his impulses will help the individual to control and

183

modify them. This self-knowledge sometimes results in the better development of the man's personality.

VIII. In the last section it was suggested that the development of homosexual tendencies could be prevented by a better understanding of their cause and that more information and training should be provided for all those people who are entrusted with the care of children. Various changes in the law and in the social attitude to homosexuality were also suggested.

Clearly it is a big problem affecting many people. These people cannot be blamed for their condition and a cure cannot be guaranteed. The existing law is ineffective in dealing with the problem and the present attitude of society is not only unenlightened, it is also indirectly responsible for producing anti-social inclinations in the confirmed homosexual and difficult maladjustments in the abstainer.

Throughout this book, hard words have been used in describing some of the injustices inflicted upon these men suffering from this mental disorder. It should be noted, however, that the strongest words have been direct quotations from high medical and legal authorities. The best medical and legal brains who have studied this problem do not need to be convinced by any of the arguments used in this book. But they cannot move towards a solution until they have the backing of a more enlightened public.

It would be a mistake to make sudden, sweeping changes, but it would be equally wrong to be content to allow things to remain as they are to-day. It is hoped that some progress will soon be made to relieve the suffering of these thousands of people even if we can only make haste slowly. In all humility it is suggested that certain things can and should be done at once.

(1) We should recognize that more research into the problem of homosexuality is urgently required.

(2) Parents, teachers, etc., should be made to see that the problem exists, and can be prevented, by recognizing the dangers and modifying the upbringing of our children.

(3) We might ask ourselves if the law as it stands to-day is either just or achieving its purpose.

(4) We might question whether the social stigma attached to homosexuality does not actually do more harm than good.

(5) We should recognize that we will not even start to find a solution until we sweep away the prudish silence and superstitious prejudices that surround the subject. The problem of homosexuality must be brought out into the open where it can be discussed and reconsidered. That is the object of this book.

REFERENCES

1. Ahrenfeldt, R. H.: "Homosexuality and Sexual Trauma", *Brit. Med. Journ.*, vol. ii, 1947.

2. Allen, C.: *The Sexual Perversions and Abnormalities*. Oxford University Press. London. 1949.

3. Archenholtz, J. W.: *England and Italy*. A. B. Soakes, Amsterdam. 1791.

4. Beccle, H. C.: *Psychiatry*. Faber and Faber. London. 1949.

5. Berkman, A.: *Prison Memoires of an Anarchist*. C. W. Daniel, London. 1926.

6. Bloch, I.: *Sexual Life in England Past and Present*. Francis Aldor, London. 1938.

7. Bloch, I.: *The Sexual Life of Our Time*. Translated by M. E. Paul. Rebman, London. 1908.

8. Brend, W.: *Sacrifice to Attis*. Heinemann, London. 1936.

9. Brill, A. A.: *The Basic Writings of Sigmund Freud*. Random House, New York. 1938.

10. Connor, W. A.: "Some Notes on Suicide", *Brit. Journ. of Med. Psy.*, vol. xxi, 1948.

11. Darwin, C.: *The Descent of Man and Selection in Relation to Sex*. C. A. Watts, London. 1930.

12. Devereux, G.: "Institutionalized Homosexuality of the Mohave Indians", *Human Biology*, vol. ix, 1937.

13. Domingo, S.: *London as It Is*. H. C. Schetsberg, Leipzig. 1826.

14. Doshay, L. J.: *The Boy Offender and His Later Career*. Grune and Stratton, New York. 1943.

15. East, N.: "Social Aspects of Homosexuality", *Medico-Legal Review*, vol. xv, 1947.

16. East, N.: "The Modern Psychological Approach to Crime", *Journ. of Ment. Science*, vol. xxxv, 1939.

17. East, N. and Hubert, W.: *Psychological Treatment of Crime*. His Majesty's Stationery Office. 1939.

18. Ellis, H.: *Studies in the Psychology of Sex*. Random House, New York. 1933.

185

19. Ellis, H.: *Sex in Relation to Society*. Heinemann, London. 1937.

20. Hooton, E. A.: quoted by Ernst and Loth in *Sexual Behaviour and the Kinsey Report*. Falcon Press, London. 1949.

21. Fenichel, O.: *Outline of Clinical Psychoanalysis*. Kegan Paul, London. 1934.

22. Ferenczi, V.: *The Role of Homosexuality in the Pathogenesis of Paranoia*. Quoted by Henderson and Gillespie in the 7th Edition of *The Textbook of Psychiatry*. Oxford University Press, London. 1950.

23. Finsch, O.: "Medical Notes from the Carolines", *Zeitschrift für Ethnologie*. E. J. Brill, Berlin. 1880.

24. Fishman, J. F.: *Sex in Prison*. National Library Press, New York. 1934.

25. Fraxi, P.: *Index librorum prohibitorum*. Quoted by Iwan Bloch in *Sexual Life in England Past and Present*. Francis Aldor, London. 1938.

26. Freeman, E.: *The Reign of William Rufus*. Oxford University Press, London. 1882.

27. Freidlander, K.: *The Psychoanalytical Approach to Juvenile Delinquency*. Routledge, London. 1947.

28. Frost, I. "Social and Legal Aspects of Sexual Abnormality", *Medical-Legal Review*, vol. xiii, 1945.

29. Freud, S.: "Notes on the Autobiography of a Paranoiac", *Collected Papers*, vol. iii. Hogarth Press, London. 1925.

30. Glass, Deuel and Wright: "Sex Hormones Studies in Male Homosexuality", *Endocrinal.*, vol. xxvi, 1940.

31. Glover, E.: "Social and Legal Aspects of Sexual Abnormality", *Medico-Legal Review*, vol. xiii, 1945.

32. Glover E.: *Psycho-Analysis*. Staples Press, London. 1949.

33. Harrison, T.: *Savage Civilization*. Gollancz, London. 1937.

34. Henry, G.: "Psychogenic Factors in Overt Homosexuality", *Am. Journ. of Psychiatry*, vol. xciii, 1937.

35. Henry, G. and Galbraith, H.: "Constitutional Factors in Homosexuality", *Am. Journ. of Psychiatry*, vol. xiii, 1934.

36. Henry, G. and Gross, S.: "Social Factors in Case Histories of a Hundred Underprivileged Homosexuals", *Am. Mental Hygiene*, vol. xxii, 1938.

37. Higden, R.: *Polychronicon Ranulphi Higden*. Rolls Series, vol. viii. Her Majesty's Stationery Office. 1882.

38. Hirschfeld, M.: *Sexual Anomalies and Perversions*. Simpkin Marshall, London. 1937.

39. Hovey, K.: "Social Aspects of Homosexuality", *Medico-Legal Review*, vol. xv, 1947.

40. Humphreys, T.: The Preface to *The Trials of Oscar Wilde*. Edited by Montgomery Hyde. Notable British Trials Series. London. 1948.

41. Hyde, H. M.: *The Trials of Oscar Wilde*. Notable British Trials Series. 1948.

42. Jenkins, M.: *Genetic Psychological Monographs*, vol. iii. Clark University Press, Worcester, Mass. 1928.

43. Karpman, B.: "Perversions as Neuroses (Paraphiliac Neuroses)", *Journ. of Crim. Psychopathology*, vol. iii, 1941.

44. Kenny C. S.: *Outlines of Criminal Law*. Cambridge University Press. Cambridge. 1944.

45. Kinsey, A., Pomeroy, W., and Martin, C.: *Sexual Behaviour in the Human Male*. W. B. Saunders, Philadelphia. 1948.

46. Krafft-Ebing, R.: "New Studies in the Domain of Homosexuality", *Annual for Sexual Intermediate Stages*, vol. iii. Leipzig. 1901.

47. Krafft-Ebing, R.: *Psychopathia sexualis*. Translation of the 12th Edition. Heinemann, London. 1939.

48. Lang, T.: "Studies in the Genetic Determination of Homosexuality", *Journ. of Nerv. and Ment. Diseases*, vol. xcii, 1940.

49. Lange, J.: *Crime as Destiny: a Study of Criminal Twins*. Translated by Charlotte Haldane. Allen and Unwin, London. 1930.

50. Liebman, S.: "Homosexuality, Transvestism and Psychosis", *Journ. of Nerv. and Ment. Disease*, vol. xcix, 1944.

51. Loeser, L. H.: "The Sexual Psychopath in Military Service", *Am. Journ. of Psychiatry*, vol. cii, 1945.

52. Lydston, G. F.: *Impotence, Sterility, and Sex Gland Implantation*. Riverton Press, Chicago. 1917.

53. Mackwood, J. C.: "Social Aspects of Homosexuality", *Medico-Legal Review*, vol. xv, 1947.

54. McPartland, J.: *Sex in Our Changing World*. Torchstream Books, New York. 1938.

55. Mead, M.: *Male and Female: a Study of the Sexes in a Changing World*. Gollancz, London. 1949.

56. Menninger, K.: "Varieties of Homosexual Manifestations", *Am. Journ. of Psychiatry*, vol. xcii, 1935.

57. Nelson, V.: *Prison Days and Nights*. Little, Brown, Boston. 1930.

58. Neustadt, R., and Myerson, A.: "Quantitative Sex Hormone Studies in Homosexuality, Childhood, and Various Neuropsychiatric Disturbances", *Am. Journ. of Psychiatry*, vol. xcvii, 1940.

59. Ovidius: *Ars Amatoria*. Translated by F. A. Wright. Routledge, London. 1924.

60. Owensby, N. M.: "Homosexuality and Lesbianism treated with Metrazol", *Journ. of Nerv. and Ment. Disease*, vol. xcii, 1940.

61. Philip, H. L.: "Homosexuality", *Brit. Med. Journ.*, April, 1946.

62. Raffalovich, M.: *Uranisme et Unisexualite*. A. Storck, Lyon. 1896.

63. Rolph, C. H.: "Prostitution and the Law", *New Statesman and Nation*, May, 1947.

64. Rosanoff, A. J.: *Manual of Psychiatry*. 7th Edition. Chapman and Hall, London. 1938.

65. Sessions Hodge, R.: "Medico-Legal Aspects of the Treatment of the Sexual Offender", *Medico-Legal Journal*, vol. xviii, 1950.

66. Stanley-Jones, D.: "Homosexuals", *Brit. Med. Journ.*, February, 1946.

67. Stanley-Jones D.: "Sexual Inversion: an Ethical Study", *The Lancet*, March, 1947.

68. Stead, W. T.: Editorial in the *Review of Reviews*, June, 1895.

69. Stekel, W.: *Compulsion and Doubt*. Peter Nevill, London. 1950.

70. Stevenson, G. S.: *The Letters of Madame*. vol. i. Chapman and Dodd, London. 1924.

71. Stürup, G. K.: "The Management and Treatment of Psychopaths in a Special Institution in Denmark", *Proc. Roy. Med.*, vol. xli, 1948.

72. Taylor, F. H.: "Homosexual Offences and Their Relation to Psychotherapy", *Brit. Med. Journ.*, October, 1947.

73. Ward, E.: *The History of London Clubs*. J. Dutten, London. 1709.

74. Walker, K.: *The Physiology of Sex*. Pelican Books, London. 1940.

75. Weininger, O.: *Sex and Character*. Heinemann, London. 1906.

76. Wilde, O.: *De Profundis*. Methuen, London. 1949.

77. Williams, E.: "Homosexuality: a Biological Anomaly", *Journ. of Nerv. and Ment. Disease*, vol. xcix, 1944.

78. Wortis, J.: "The Body Build of the Male Homosexual", *Am. Journ. of Psychiatry*, vol. xciii, 1937.

79. *Yokel's Preceptor: or More Sprees in London*. H. Smith, London. 1850.

80. Zilboorg, G., and Henry, G.: *History of Medical Psychology*. Allen and Unwin, London. 1941.

BIBLIOGRAPHY

*A short bibliography of the principal works
not otherwise referred to in the text*

Alexander, F.: *Fundamentals of Psychoanalysis*. Allen and Unwin, London. 1950.

Allen, C.: *Modern Discoveries in Medical Psychology*. Macmillan, London. 1937.

Bleuler, E.: *Textbook of Psychiatry*. Macmillan, New York. 1924.

Brend, W.: *Traumatic Mental Disorders in Courts of Law*. Heinemann, London. 1938.

Dollard, J., and Miller, N.; *Personality and Psychotherapy*. McGraw-Hill, New York. 1950.

Fairbairn, W. R.: "The Psychological Aspects of Sexual Delinquency", *Mental Hygiene*, vol. v. 1939.

Finger, F. W.: "Sexual Beliefs among College Students", *Journ. of Abnorm. and Soc. Psychology*, vol. xlii, 1947.

Freud, S.: *Collected Works*. Hogarth Press, London. 1924.

Freud, S.: *Three Contributions to the Theory of Sex*. Nervous and Mental Disease Publications, Washington. 1930.

Glass and Johnson: "Limitations of Organotherapy in Homosexuals", *Journ. of Clin. Endocr.*, vol. xi, 1944.

Greenspan and Campbell: "The Homosexual as a Personality Type", *Am. Journ. of Psychiatry*, vol. ci, 1945.

Guyon, R.: *Sex Life and Ethics*. Translated by J. and I. Flugel. John Lane The Bodley Head, London. 1933.

Henderson and Gillespie: *Textbook of Psychiatry*. 7th Edition. Oxford University Press, London. 1950.

Henry, G.: *Sex Variants*. Paul B. Hoeber, New York. 1941.

Kraines, S. H.: *The Therapy of the Neuroses and Psychoses*. Kimpton, London. 1948.

Lowrey, L. G.: *Psychiatry for Social Workers*. Oxford University Press, London. 1950.

Mead, M.: *Sex and Temperament in Three Primitive Societies*. Routledge, London. 1935.

Rennie and Woodward: *Mental Health in Modern Society*. Commonwealth Fund Publications, New York. 1948.

Rosanoff, A. J.: "A Theory of Chaotic Sexuality", *Am. Journ. of Psychiatry*, vol. xcii, 1935.

Sprague, G.: "Varieties of Homosexual Manifestations", *Am. Journ. of Psychiatry*, vol. xcii, 1935.

Stekel, W.: *The Homosexual Neuroses*. Emerson, New York. 1933.

Stott, D. H.: *Delinquency and Human Nature*. Carnegie U.K. Trust, Dunfermline. 1950.

Thorner, M. W.: *Psychiatry in General Practice*. W. B. Saunders, Philadelphia. 1948.

Walker and Strauss: *Sexual Disorders in the Male*. Hamish Hamilton, London. 1939.

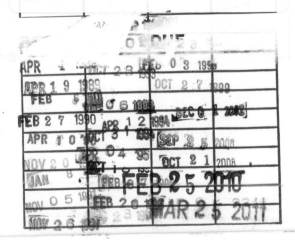